Legalines

Editorial Advisors:

Gloria A. Aluise
   Attorney at Law
Jonathan Neville
   Attorney at Law
Robert A. Wyler
   Attorney at Law

Authors:

Gloria A. Aluise
   Attorney at Law
Daniel O. Bernstine
   Attorney at Law
Roy L. Brooks
   Professor of Law
Scott M. Burbank
   C.P.A.
Charles N. Carnes
   Professor of Law
Paul S. Dempsey
   Professor of Law
Jerome A. Hoffman
   Professor of Law
Mark R. Lee
   Professor of Law
Jonathan Neville
   Attorney at Law
Laurence C. Nolan
   Professor of Law
Arpiar Saunders
   Attorney at Law
Robert A. Wyler
   Attorney at Law

WILLS, TRUSTS & ESTATES

Adaptable to Seventh Edition* of Dukeminier Casebook

By Gloria A. Aluise
Attorney at Law

*If your casebook is a newer edition, go to www.gilbertlaw.com
to see if a supplement is available for this title.

THOMSON

WEST

EDITORIAL OFFICE: 1 N. Dearborn Street, Suite 650, Chicago, IL 60602
REGIONAL OFFICES: Chicago, Dallas, Los Angeles, New York, Washington, D.C.

SERIES EDITOR
Linda C. Schneider, J.D.
Attorney at Law

PRODUCTION MANAGER
Elizabeth G. Duke

SECOND PRINTING—2008

Legalines®

**Features Detailed Briefs of Every Major Case,
Plus Summaries of the Black Letter Law**

Titles Available

Administrative Law .... Keyed to Breyer	Criminal Law .... Keyed to Dressler
Administrative Law .... Keyed to Schwartz	Criminal Law .... Keyed to Johnson
Administrative Law .... Keyed to Strauss	Criminal Law .... Keyed to Kadish
Antitrust .... Keyed to Areeda	Criminal Law .... Keyed to Kaplan
Antitrust .... Keyed to Pitofsky	Criminal Law .... Keyed to LaFave
Business Associations .... Keyed to Klein	Criminal Procedure .... Keyed to Kamisar
Civil Procedure .... Keyed to Friedenthal	Domestic Relations .... Keyed to Wadlington
Civil Procedure .... Keyed to Hazard	Estates & Trusts .... Keyed to Dobris
Civil Procedure .... Keyed to Yeazell	Evidence .... Keyed to Mueller
Conflict of Laws .... Keyed to Currie	Evidence .... Keyed to Waltz
Constitutional Law .... Keyed to Brest	Family Law .... Keyed to Areen
Constitutional Law .... Keyed to Choper	Income Tax .... Keyed to Freeland
Constitutional Law .... Keyed to Cohen	Income Tax .... Keyed to Klein
Constitutional Law .... Keyed to Rotunda	Labor Law .... Keyed to Cox
Constitutional Law .... Keyed to Stone	Property .... Keyed to Cribbet
Constitutional Law .... Keyed to Sullivan	Property .... Keyed to Dukeminier
Contracts .... Keyed to Calamari	Property .... Keyed to Nelson
Contracts .... Keyed to Dawson	Property .... Keyed to Rabin
Contracts .... Keyed to Farnsworth	Remedies .... Keyed to Rendelman
Contracts .... Keyed to Fuller	Securities Regulation .... Keyed to Coffee
Contracts .... Keyed to Kessler	Torts .... Keyed to Dobbs
Contracts .... Keyed to Knapp	Torts .... Keyed to Epstein
Contracts .... Keyed to Murphy	Torts .... Keyed to Franklin
Corporations .... Keyed to Choper	Torts .... Keyed to Henderson
Corporations .... Keyed to Eisenberg	Torts .... Keyed to Prosser
Corporations .... Keyed to Hamilton	Wills, Trusts & Estates .... Keyed to Dukeminier

All Titles Available at Your Law School Bookstore

THOMSON
™
WEST

SHORT SUMMARY OF CONTENTS

TABLE OF CONTENTS AND SHORT REVIEW OUTLINE

I. INTRODUCTION TO ESTATE PLANNING

A. PROLOGUE

The material in this outline covers wills, trusts, future interests, and estate and trust administration. Each of these topics relates to the social process by which private wealth is transmitted and allocated, and each is critical to a comprehensive understanding of the estate planning process.

B. THE POWER TO TRANSMIT PROPERTY AT DEATH AND ITS LIMITATIONS

1. **T. Jefferson.** "The earth belongs in usufruct to the living; the dead have neither powers nor rights over it."

2. **2 W. Blackstone, Commentaries.** "The permanent right of property, vested in the ancestor himself, was [not a] *natural*, but merely a *civil* right." "Wills . . . testaments, rights of inheritance[,] and successions are all . . . creatures of the civil or municipal laws."

3. **Supreme Court.** In *Irving Trust Co. v. Day*, 314 U.S. 556 (1942), the Supreme Court held that succession rights to a deceased person's property are created by statute. The Constitution does not forbid state legislatures from limiting or abolishing testamentary disposition over property.

4. **Taking Property Without Just Compensation--**

Hodel v. Irving, 481 U.S. 704 (1987).

Facts. Pursuant to an 1889 act of Congress, tracts of land reserved for the Sioux Indian Nation were allotted to individual Sioux, although held in trust by the United States, and were allowed to pass to the allottees' heirs. Succeeding generations of Sioux divided their predecessors' tracts into increasingly tiny undivided fractional interests, which often yielded pennies in annual rent. Congress responded by enacting section 207 of the Indian Land Consolidation Act of 1983, which provided that any undivided fractional interest representing less than 2% of a tract's acreage, and which had earned less than $100 in the preceding year, would escheat to the tribe rather than descend by intestacy or devise. Three Sioux who would have inherited such interests but for the operation of section 207 filed an action for injunctive and declaratory relief in federal court, claiming that section 207 violated the Fifth Amendment by taking private property without just compensation.

The District Court found that the heirs (Ps) did not have any vested property interest which would be entitled to constitutional protection, and accordingly denied relief. The Eighth Circuit reversed, holding that: (i) Ps had standing to assert the decedents' right to control the disposition of their property, and (ii) the taking of that right without compensation violated the Fifth Amendment.

Issue. Does a federal statute barring inheritance of Indian land allotments and providing for escheat to the tribe effect a taking of the decedents' property without just compensation in violation of the Fifth Amendment?

Held. Yes. Judgment affirmed.

♦ The fact that section 207 has deprived those tribal members of fractional interests that they would otherwise have inherited is sufficient injury in fact to satisfy the case or controversy requirement of Article III of the United States Constitution.

♦ The original version of section 207 of the Indian Land Consolidation Act of 1983 effects a taking of property without just compensation in violation of the Fifth Amendment. It entirely abolishes both the descent and devise of these property interests even when the passing of the property to an heir might result in the consolidation of property.

♦ The government has considerable latitude, under the Just Compensation Clause of the Fifth Amendment, in regulating property rights in ways that may adversely affect the owners.

♦ There is no set formula for determining when justice and fairness require that economic injuries caused by public action be compensated by the government, rather than remaining disproportionately concentrated on a few persons. Instead, the question whether such action results in a taking of property under the Fifth Amendment is examined by engaging in essentially ad hoc, factual inquiries in which several factors—such as the economic impact of the regulation, its interference with reasonable investment-backed expectations, and the character of the governmental action—have particular significance.

♦ Although the state and federal governments have broad authority to adjust the rules governing the descent and devise of property without implicating the guarantees of the Just Compensation Clause of the Fifth Amendment, the complete abolition of both the descent and devise of a particular class of property may constitute a taking within the meaning of that clause. Under these facts, both descent and devise are abolished even where the governmental purpose sought to be advanced, consolidation of ownership of Indian lands, does not conflict with the further descent of the property.

5. Partial Restraints on Marriage Permissible--

Shapira v. Union National Bank, 315 N.E.2d 825 (Ohio 1974).

Facts. The will of the decedent, David Shapira, M.D., bequeathed a portion of the residue of his estate to his son, Daniel Jacob Shapira (P), provided that he is married to a Jewish girl, both of whose parents are Jewish, at the time of the testator's death. If after seven years from the testator's death, P is unmarried or married to a non-Jewish girl, then his share should go to the State of Israel. P, who is 21 years old and unmarried, brings a petition in the Court of Common Pleas for a declaratory judgment, arguing that the condition upon his inheritance is unconstitutional, contrary to public policy, and unenforceable because of its unreasonableness.

Issues.

(i)   Is a partial restraint on marriage in a will a violation of the right to marry protected by the Fourteenth Amendment?

(ii)   Is a partial restraint on marriage that imposes only reasonable restrictions valid and not contrary to public policy?

Held. (i) No. (ii) Yes. Petition denied.

◆   P is correct that the right to marry is constitutionally protected from restrictive state legislative action. Here, however, the court is not asked to enforce any restriction on P's constitutional right to marry; rather, the court is asked to enforce the testator's restriction on his son's inheritance. The right to receive property is a creature of the law and is not a constitutionally guaranteed right. Hence, upholding the partial restraint imposed by the testator will not violate the Constitution.

◆   Nor does a partial restraint on marriage violate public policy. If the condition were that the beneficiary not marry anyone, the restraint would be general or total and would be held contrary to public policy. A partial restraint on marriage that imposes only reasonable restrictions is valid, and not contrary to public policy. The weight of authority in the United States is that gifts conditioned on the beneficiary's marrying within a particular religious class or faith are reasonable. It is the conclusion of this court that the conditions contained in the testator's will are reasonable restrictions on marriage and are valid.

C. THE PROBATE PROCESS

1.   **Introduction and Terminology.** The general steps in the probate process are (i) opening the estate by offering the will for probate, (ii) collecting the decedent's

assets, (iii) paying any family allowance and setting aside homestead and exempt personal property, (iv) paying creditors' claims and tax bills, and (v) distributing the assets of the estate upon the probate court entering a decree of distribution.

a. **Executor, administrator.** The executor is a personal representative named in a will. The administrator is a personal representative appointed by the court. There are various types of administrators.

1) **Administrator.** An administrator is a person originally appointed when the decedent dies intestate.

2) **Administrator with the will annexed (administrator c.t.a.).** An administrator with the will annexed (administrator c.t.a.) is a person appointed when the decedent dies testate but no executor is named in the will.

3) **Administrator of goods not administered (administered d.b.n.).** An administrator of goods not administered (administered d.b.n.) is a person appointed to succeed an original administrator.

4) **Administrator c.t.a.d.b.n.** An administrator c.t.a.d.b.n. is a person appointed to succeed an executor or an administrator c.t.a.

5) **Special administrator.** A special administrator is a person appointed to preserve the assets pending qualification of the regular administrator.

b. **Other terminology.** The terminology used in decedents' estates and trusts originated primarily in England, where common law courts had jurisdiction over real property and ecclesiastical courts had jurisdiction over personal property. Each group developed a distinct terminology that has carried over to this day. Some key terms are defined below.

1) **Succession.** Succession is the process of becoming beneficially entitled to the property of a decedent.

2) **Intestate succession.** Intestate succession occurs when the decedent leaves no valid will, so that his property passes to those of his relatives named in a state statute (called the intestate law).

3) **Statute of descent.** A statute of descent is an intestate law that applies only to real property. Intestate real property is said to pass by descent.

4) **Statute of distribution.** A statute of distribution is an intestate law that applies only to personal property. Intestate personal property is said to pass by distribution.

5) **Statute of descent and distribution.** A statute of descent and distribution is an intestate law that applies to both real and personal property.

6) **Heir.** A person entitled by statute to the land of the intestate is called the heir or heir at law.

   a) **Expectant heir.** An expectant heir is one who expects to take by inheritance.

   b) **Prospective heir.** A prospective heir is one who may inherit but may be excluded. This category includes heirs presumptive and heirs apparent.

      (1) **Heir presumptive.** An heir presumptive is a person who will inherit if the potential intestate dies immediately, but who will be excluded if relatives closer in relationship are born.

      (2) **Heir apparent.** An heir apparent is one who is certain to inherit unless excluded by a valid will.

7) **Next of kin (or distributee).** The next of kin, or distributee, is that person (or persons) who is, or may be, entitled to the personal property of an intestate. This person is said to *inherit* the personal property.

8) **Ascendant or ancestor.** An ascendant or ancestor is a person related to an intestate or to a claimant to an intestate share in the ascending lineal line.

9) **Descendant.** A descendant is a person related to an intestate or to a claimant to an intestate share in the descending lineal line.

10) **Collateral.** A collateral is a relative who traces relationship to an intestate through a common ancestor but who is not in his lineal line of ascent or descent.

   a) **Collaterals of the half blood.** A collateral of the half blood is a person related to an intestate through only one common ancestor.

11) **Affinity.** Relationship by marriage is called affinity.

12) **Consanguinity.** Relationship by blood is called consanguinity.

13) **Escheat.** Property escheats to the state if no relatives of the intestate are entitled to inheritance.

14) **Will.** A will is an expression, either written or oral, of a person's intention concerning the disposition of property at death. A person who dies leaving a valid will is said to die *testate*.

15) **Devise.** A devise is a clause directing the disposition of real property in a will, and the person who is named to take the real property is called the devisee.

16) **Legacy.** A legacy is a clause in a will directing the disposition of money.

17) **Bequest.** A bequest is a clause in a will directing the disposition of personal property other than money.

18) **Attested, holographic, and nuncupative wills.** An attested will is a will signed by a witness. A holographic will is a will entirely in the handwriting of the testator. A nuncupative will is an oral will.

19) **Codicil.** A codicil is a testamentary instrument ancillary to a will.

20) **Probate.** Probate is the procedure by which a transaction alleged to be a will is established judicially as a valid testamentary disposition, and also applies to the act of approving the will after probate has taken place.

2. **Is Probate Necessary?** One of the primary functions of the probate process is to provide evidence of transfer of title to the decedent's heirs or devisees. However, in view of the costs and delays of probate, one may wish to avoid probate by transferring title to property during life. Three common ways of avoiding probate are (i) taking title in joint tenancy, (ii) creating a trust during life, and (iii) designating a payable-on-death beneficiary in a life insurance contract or other contract. Statutes in all states permit heirs to avoid probate where the amount of property involved is small.

3. **A Summary of Probate Procedure.**

   a. **Opening probate.** Primary or domiciliary jurisdiction is found in the jurisdiction where the decedent was domiciled at the time of death. Ancillary administration is required if the property is located in another jurisdiction. Each state has a detailed statutory procedure for issuance of letters testamentary or letters of administration. The majority of states require prior notice to interested parties before the appointment of a personal representative or probate of a will. Under the Uniform Probate Code ("UPC"), the representative also has a duty to publish a newspaper notice for creditors once each week for three weeks.

   b. **Supervising the representative's actions.** The probate court supervises the representative's actions and approves the inventory and appraisal, payment of debts, family allowance, granting of options on real estate, borrowing of funds, personal representative's commissions, attorneys' fees, preliminary and final distributions, and discharge of the personal representative.

  c. Closing the estate. The representative is under a fiduciary duty to the estate until the court grants discharge.

4. Contest of Wills.

  a. Grounds for contest. A will contest poses the issue of whether the document offered for probate is a valid will. While most will contests involve the issues of testamentary capacity or undue influence, a will contest may also be based on defective execution, revocation of the will by the testator, lack of testamentary intent, fraud, and mistake.

D. PROFESSIONAL RESPONSIBILITY

No lawyer should prepare a will unless he considers himself competent to do so.

1. Will Beneficiaries Owed Duty of Care--

Simpson v. Calivas, 650 A.2d 318 (N.H. 1994).

Facts. Robert Simpson, Sr. (T) executed a will drafted by Christopher Calivas (D). All real estate was left to Robert Simpson, Jr. (P), except for a life estate in "our homestead located at Piscataqua Road," which was left to P's stepmother. Upon T's death, P and his stepmother filed a petition to determine whether "homestead" referred to the house and surrounding (limited) acreage or if it referred to the house, over 100 acres, buildings, and the family business on Piscataqua Road. The court admitted extrinsic evidence showing the close relationship between T and his wife, but did not admit notes taken by D during consultation with T, which read, "House to wife as a life estate remainder to son . . . remaining land . . . to son. . . ." The court construed the will to provide the stepmother with a life estate in all of the real property. Two years later, P bought out his stepmother's life estate for $400,000. P brought this malpractice action in contract, based on a third-party beneficiary theory and negligence. The trial court directed a verdict, granted D summary judgment, and dismissed. P appeals.

Issues.

(i) Does an attorney who drafts a will owe a duty to the intended beneficiary?

(ii) Did the trial court err in ruling that the findings of the probate court on the testator's intent collaterally estopped P from bringing a malpractice action?

Held. (i) Yes. (ii) Yes. Judgment reversed and case remanded.

♦ A drafting attorney owes a duty of care to an intended beneficiary, notwithstanding lack of privity, due to the foreseeability of injury to the intended beneficiary. After the testator's death, the failure of his testamentary scheme works only to deprive his intended beneficiaries of the intended bequests.

♦ If a testator contracts with an attorney to draft a will and has identified those to whom he wishes his estate to pass, the identified beneficiaries may enforce the contract as third-party beneficiaries.

♦ Where the terms of the will are ambiguous, extrinsic evidence of the testator's intent may be admitted to probate proceedings to the extent that it does not contradict the express terms of the will. While both the probate court and the superior court are competent to consider the same evidence on the issue of T's intent, that is not dispositive of an identity of issues. The probate court's role is to determine the testator's intent expressed in the language of the will. Direct declarations of the testator's intent are generally inadmissible in probate proceedings. A finding of actual intent is not necessary (or essential) to that judgment. Even an explicit finding of actual intent by a probate court cannot be the basis of collateral estoppel. Collateral estoppel is only applicable if the finding in the first proceeding was essential to the judgment of that court. [Restatement (Second) Judgments, §27]

2. Fiduciary Duty--

Hotz v. Minyard, 403 S.E.2d 634 (S.C. 1991).

Facts. Judy Minyard Hotz (P) and Tommy Minyard (D1) are brother and sister. D1 has been in charge of their father's Greenville car dealership since 1977; P worked at their father's Anderson dealership since 1983 and was also vice-president and minority shareholder. In 1985, their father signed a contract with General Motors designating P successor of the Anderson dealership.

In October of 1984, their father had Dobson (D2), a lawyer and nonpracticing CPA, draft a will, which their father executed one morning in the presence of his wife, his secretary, and D1. D1 was left the Greenville dealership; other family members were left bequests totaling $250,000 and the remainder of the estate was divided between D1 and a trust for P after the wife's death. Later the same afternoon, their father signed a second will with all of the same provisions except it gave the real estate on which the Greenville dealership was located to D1 outright. He told D2 not to disclose the existence of the second will and specifically said P should not be told about it. Three months later, P asked to see the will and with her father's permission, D2 showed her the first will and discussed it with her in detail. P claims D2 gave her the impression she would receive the Anderson dealership and said she would share equally with D1 in their father's estate. D2 claims he explained that their father intended to provide for P as he had for D1 when and if she became capable of handling a dealership. D2 noted this on the will and P claimed she thought these notes were part of the will.

About 16 months later, the father had a stroke and he is now mentally incompetent. P and D1 agreed that while their father was ill, P would care for him and D1 would temporarily run the Anderson dealership. Under D1's direction, the Anderson dealership bought another dealership, which was operating at a loss; D1 also formed a holding company, which assumed ownership of the father's real estate leased to the Anderson dealership and greatly increased the rent. When P tried to return, D1 refused to relinquish control and eventually fired her.

After P consulted another attorney, the father executed a codicil removing P and her children as beneficiaries under his will and advised P of this by letter. Later, at a meeting with their mother, D1, and D2, P was told she would be restored under the will and could work at the Greenville dealership if she dropped her plans for a lawsuit. P discharged her lawyers and moved to Greenville. Eventually, D1 terminated her.

P sued D1, D2, D2's law firm, and an accounting firm of which D2 is a shareholder and director but from which he receives no remuneration as an employee. The causes of action against D1 for tortious interference with contract, a shareholder derivative suit for wrongful diversion of corporate profits, and fraud survived summary judgment and are not at issue here. P appeals various causes of action that did not survive summary judgment, but the only issue addressed here is the trial judge's order granting summary judgment on the cause of action against D2 for breach of fiduciary duty.

Issue. Do material issues of fact, precluding summary judgment, exist as to whether D2 owed a fiduciary duty toward P, who consulted him regarding the terms of her father's will?

Held. Yes. Judgment reversed in part, affirmed in part.

♦ D2's law firm had prepared P's tax returns for approximately 20 years until 1985 and had prepared a will for her which she had signed only one week before she inquired about the effect of her father's will. P testified she had consulted D2 in 1984 or 1985 about a suspected misappropriation of funds at one of the dealerships and as late as 1986 about her problems with D1. A fiduciary relationship exists when one has a special confidence in another so that the latter, in equity and good conscience, is bound to act in good faith.

♦ An attorney-client relationship is a fiduciary one. D2 did not owe P a duty to disclose the existence of the second will, but he did owe her a duty to deal with her in good faith and not actively misrepresent the first will.

♦ Since D2 was acting as an attorney when he met with P, there is evidence to present a jury issue whether D2's law firm should be held vicariously liable for D2's conduct.

II. INTESTACY: AN ESTATE PLAN BY DEFAULT

A. THE BASIC SCHEME

All states have statutes of descent and distribution that govern the distribution of the property of a person who dies intestate, or who does not make a complete distribution of the estate. Generally, the law of the state where the decedent was domiciled at death governs the disposition of personal property, and the law of the state where the decedent's real property is located governs the disposition of his real property.

1. **Spouse.** Under common law, a spouse was not an heir and the decedent's property passed by intestacy to descendants. Today, the surviving spouse takes an intestate share of the decedent's estate in all jurisdictions. If the decedent is survived by a spouse and by descendants (children, grandchildren, etc.), in most states the spouse takes one-third or one-half of the decedent's estate. If the decedent is survived by a spouse but not by descendants or parents, in many states the spouse inherits the entire estate.

   a. **Simultaneous death.** A person cannot take as an heir or will beneficiary unless he survives the decedent for at least an instant of time. However, it is often difficult to determine whether the person survived the decedent (*e.g.,* when the person and the decedent are both fatally injured in an accident). The Uniform Simultaneous Death Act (or its Uniform Probate Code ("UPC") equivalent, the 120-hour survival rule) provides for this situation. Under the Act, where the title to property or the devolution thereof depends upon priority of death and there is no sufficient evidence that the parties have died otherwise than simultaneously, the property of each person shall be disposed of as if he had survived. If there is sufficient evidence that one party survived the other, even for a brief period of time, the Act does not apply.

      1) **Evidence of survival--**

Janus v. Tarasewicz, 482 N.E.2d 418 (Ill. 1985).

Facts. This declaratory judgment action arose out of the deaths of a husband and wife who died after ingesting Tylenol capsules laced with cyanide. Stanley Janus was pronounced dead shortly after he was admitted to the hospital. However, Theresa Janus was placed on life support systems for almost two days before being pronounced dead. Claiming that there was not sufficient evidence that Theresa Janus survived her husband, Stanley's mother (P) brought this action for the proceeds of Stanley's $100,000 life insurance policy, which named Theresa as the primary beneficiary and P as the contingent beneficiary.

Metropolitan Life Insurance Company (D1) paid the proceeds to Tarasewicz (D2), who is Theresa's father and the administrator of her estate. The trial court found sufficient evidence that Theresa survived Stanley. P and the administrator of Stanley's estate appealed, contending that there is not sufficient evidence to prove that both victims did not suffer brain death prior to their arrival at the hospital.

Issue. In a factually disputed case of whether one spouse survived the other, is the appellate court's review limited to whether the trial court's finding was against the manifest weight of the evidence?

Held. Yes. Judgment affirmed.

♦　　A civil case is governed by the law as it exists when a judgment is rendered, not when the facts underlying the case occur.

♦　　Even though *In re Haymer*, which set forth standards for determining when legal death occurs, was decided after the deaths in issue, the trial court properly applied the *Haymer* standards. Furthermore, application of those standards was not unfair since the treating physicians had made pertinent diagnoses at the time of the deaths and the parties presented evidence relevant under the standards.

♦　　Survivorship is a fact that must be proven by a preponderance of the evidence by the party whose claim depends on survivorship.

♦　　In cases where survivorship is determined by the testimony of lay witnesses, the burden of sufficient evidence may be met by evidence of a positive sign of life in one body and the absence of any such sign in the other.

♦　　In cases where the death process is monitored by medical professionals, their testimony as to the usual and customary standards of medical practice are highly relevant when considering what constitutes a positive sign of life and what constitutes a criterion for determining death.

♦　　The appellate court's task on review of a factually disputed case is to determine whether the trial court's finding was against the manifest weight of the evidence. The finding here that the wife survived her husband was not against the manifest weight of the evidence.

―――――――――――――

2.　**Descendants.**

　　a.　**Taking by representation: per stirpes distribution.** After the spouse's share is set aside, the children and the issue of deceased children of the decedent will take the remainder of the decedent's property. If the decedent is survived by children and grandchildren, the grandchildren will take a share of the estate only if they are children of a deceased child of the decedent. Grandchildren take only by representation.

       1)   **UPC rule—per capita at each generation.** UPC section 2-106 provides that each descendant at the first generational level at which there are living takers takes one share, and the share of each deceased person at that generational level is divided equally among the descendants at the next generational level.

       2)   **Minority rule—strict per stirpes.** A few states apply a "strict per stirpes" rule. Under this rule, the stirpital shares are always determined at the first generational level, even if there are no living takers at that level.

    3.   **Ancestors and Collaterals.** If the intestate is survived by descendants, parents and collaterals do not take in any jurisdiction. If there are no descendants, the intestate's property is usually distributed to the parents after deducting the spouse's share. In nearly all states, if the intestate is not survived by a spouse, descendants, or parents, the estate passes to the descendants of the intestate's parents, *i.e.,* to the decedent's brothers and sisters (and the descendants of deceased brothers and sisters, per stirpes).

       a.   **Half bloods.** In most states, a relative of the half blood (*e.g.,* a half-brother) is treated the same as a relative of the whole blood.

       b.   **Escheat.** If there are no heirs, the property of the decedent escheats to the state in all jurisdictions.

B.   TRANSFERS TO CHILDREN

    1.   **Meaning of Children.**

       a.   **Adopted children.** In all states that have enacted statutes governing inheritance rights of adopted children, an adopted child has the same inheritance rights as a natural child.

       1)   **Loss of inheritance rights from or through natural parents--**

Hall v. Vallandingham, 540 A.2d 1162 (Md. 1988).

Facts. Earl Vallandingham died in 1956, survived by his widow, Elizabeth, and their four children. Two years later, Elizabeth married Jim Killgore, who adopted the children. Earl's brother, William, died childless, unmarried, and intestate. His sole heirs were his surviving brothers and sisters and the children of the brothers and sisters who predeceased him. Earl's four natural children (Ps) alleged that they were entitled to the distributive share of their natural uncle William's estate that their natural father would have received had he survived. The circuit court found that Ps were not entitled to inherit from the decedent because of their adoption by their stepfather after the death of their natural father and the remarriage of their natural mother. Ps appeal.

Issue. Do children adopted after the death of a natural parent lose all rights of inheritance from or through that natural parent?

Held. Yes. Judgment affirmed.

- Every state possesses the power to regulate the manner by which property within its dominion may be transmitted by will or inheritance and to prescribe who can receive that property. The state may deny the privilege altogether or may impose whatever restrictions upon the grant it deems appropriate.

- An adopted child is entitled to all of the rights and privileges of a biological child insofar as the adoptive parents are concerned, but adoption does not confer upon the adopted child more rights and privileges than those possessed by a natural child. To allow dual inheritance would bestow upon an adopted child a superior status.

- Adopted children may not inherit from or through their natural parents. Once a child is adopted, the rights of both the natural parents and their relatives are terminated.

- Because an adopted child has no right to inherit from the estate of a natural parent who dies intestate, it follows that the same child may not inherit through the natural parent by way of representation.

---

2)   Adopted adult not considered an "heir"--

Minary v. Citizens Fidelity Bank & Trust Co., 419 S.W.2d 340 (Ky. 1967).

Facts. The will of the decedent, Amelia S. Minary (T), devised her residuary estate in trust to pay the income to her husband and three sons for their respective lives. The trust was to terminate upon the death of the last surviving beneficiary, at which time the trust was to be distributed to T's surviving heirs and if no heirs, then to the First Christian Church. Two of the three sons left no surviving issues, but a third son, Alfred, married and thereafter adopted his wife. Myra Minary (P) the wife of Alfred, brought suit against the Citizens Fidelity Bank (D), contending that the trust should be awarded to her since she, having been adopted by her husband, becomes an "heir" for purposes of the will. The trial court held for P. D appeals.

Issue. Will adoption of an adult for the purpose of bringing that person under the provisions of a preexisting testamentary instrument be permitted?

Held. No. Judgment reversed.

- Even though the adoption statute provides that an adult person may be adopted in the same manner as a child, we are constrained to view this practice as an act of subterfuge that thwarts the testator's intent. Here, were we to give strict effect to the adoption statute, we would thwart the efforts of the deceased to dispose of her property as she saw fit. Adoption of an adult for the purpose of bringing that person under the provisions of a preexisting testamentary instrument when she clearly was not intended to be so covered should not be permitted, and we do not view this as doing any great violence to our adoption laws.

Comment. The cases are split over whether individuals who are adopted as adults should be treated as descendants. In *Commerce Bank v. Blasdel*, 141 S.W.3d 434 (Mo. 2004), the court held that six stepchildren who were adopted as adults were the descendants of the adopting parents' parents and, therefore, were entitled to share in trusts created by their grandparents.

---

3) **Equitable adoption.** The doctrine of "equitable adoption," based on estoppel principles, allows a child to inherit from a stepparent or foster parent just as though the child had been adopted. The basis of the estoppel is the stepparent's or foster parent's conduct in failing to perform the agreement to adopt. The doctrine only works against the stepparent or foster parent. Thus, if there is an unperformed agreement to adopt and the child dies intestate, the stepparent or foster parent does not inherit from the child.

a) **No valid adoption--**

O'Neal v. Wilkes, 439 S.E.2d 490 (Ga. 1994).

Facts. O'Neal (P) filed a petition in equity seeking a declaration of virtual adoption. P was given to the Cooks by her aunt in 1961. P lived with the Cooks and after they were divorced, continued to live with Mr. Cook until 1975 when P was married. P was educated by Mr. Cook and he identified P's children as his grandchildren. When Mr. Cook died, his administrator, Wilkes (D), refused to recognize P's asserted interest in Mr. Cook's estate. A jury found P had been virtually adopted. The court granted a judgment n.o.v., finding that P's aunt was without authority to contract for P's adoption. P appeals.

Issue. Does an aunt have authority to contract for her niece's adoption if she is not the legal guardian?

Held. No. Judgment affirmed.

♦ Although P's father had never acknowledged P and his consent to the adoption was not necessary, P's aunt was not P's "legal guardian."

♦ Even though P's aunt had physical possession of P at the time of the adoption, P's aunt was not given legal custody by court order; even if she had been "legal custodian," under Georgia law, a custodian does not have the right to consent to a child's adoption.

Dissent. Equity considers that done which ought to have been done. This court has held that an agreement to adopt a child, so as to make the child an heir on the adopting person's death, performed on the part of the child, is enforceable upon the death of the adopting person as to property undisposed of by the will. P has fully performed the alleged contract over a lifetime.

---

b. **Posthumous children.** Today, in many states, a child conceived during the father's lifetime but born after his death is considered his child for inheritance purposes.

c. **Nonmarital children.** In all states today, a child born out of wedlock (*i.e.*, a nonmarital child) inherits from his natural mother and the mother's kin, and they can inherit from and through the child. While the rules respecting inheritance from the father vary, most states have adopted the provisions in UPC section 2-109, which permit paternity to be established by evidence of the parents' subsequent marriage, by the father's acknowledgment by an adjudication during the father's lifetime, or by clear and convincing proof after his death.

d. **Posthumously conceived children--**

Woodward v. Commissioner of Social Security, 760 N.E.2d 257 (Mass. 2002).

Facts. Three years after they were married, the Woodwards, childless, were told that the husband had leukemia and that treatments might leave him sterile. The couple arranged to have the husband's sperm preserved. After an unsuccessful bone marrow transplant, the husband died in 1993. In 1995, the wife gave birth to twin girls conceived through artificial insemination with the husband's sperm. In 1996, the wife applied for "child's" and "mother's" Social Security survivor benefits. The Social Security Administration ("SSA") rejected the claims on the ground that the wife had not established that the twins were the husband's "children" within the meaning of the Social Security Act, and they were not entitled to inherit from the husband under Massachusetts intestacy and paternity laws. After the wife appealed to the federal district court, seeking a declaratory judgment to reverse the SSA's ruling, that court certified the question to the Supreme Judicial Court of Massachusetts. The question is dispositive of the case and there is no precedent.

Issue. May posthumously conceived genetic children enjoy inheritance rights under the Massachusetts intestacy statute?

Held. Yes, in certain limited circumstances.

♦ The first determination that must be made is whether the twins are the issue of the husband and whether they would take under the state's intestacy laws. There are three major state interests: (i) the best interests of the children; (ii) the orderly administration of estates; and (iii) the reproductive rights of the genetic parent.

♦ The legislature has expressed that all children be afforded the same rights and protections of the law, regardless of the "accidents" of their birth. The legislature has affirmatively supported the assistive reproductive technologies that make posthumous children possible. Thus, we may assume that the legislature intended that these children be "entitled" to the same rights and protections of the law as children conceived before death.

♦ To provide certainty to heirs and creditors through the prompt, orderly, and accurate administration of intestate estates, the inheritance rights of posthumously conceived children must be determined in a timely manner, since they will reduce the share available to children conceived before the decedent's death. First, a judgment of paternity must be obtained. Second, a period of limitations must be established. Because it is undisputed in this case that the husband is the genetic father, and since the parties here stipulated that timeliness was not an issue, we will not address these concerns.

♦ There is a further consideration—that of honoring individuals' reproductive choices. The donor parent must consent to both posthumous reproduction and support of any resulting child. After the donor's death, the burden of proving the deceased genetic parent's affirmative consent to these requirements rests with the surviving parent or the legal representative. Without this proof, a court cannot be certain that the intestacy statute's goal of fraud prevention is satisfied. This certified question does not require that we determine what proof is sufficient or whether the wife has met her burden of proof.

♦ Posthumously conceived genetic children may inherit if, within time limitations, the surviving parent establishes their genetic relationship with the decedent and shows that the decedent consented both to reproduce posthumously and to support any resulting child. In any action brought to establish such inheritance rights, notice must be given to all parties.

---

2. **Advancements.** At common law and in a number of states today, any lifetime gift to a child is presumed to be an advancement of that child's intestate share to be taken into account in distributing the intestate's property at death. Many states have statutes governing advancements. Most of these statutes provide that an advancement can be made to any heir and not just a child or other descendant. The most important effect of these statutes is to reverse the common law presumption: in many states, a lifetime gift to an heir can be treated as an advancement only if (i) expressly declared as such in a writing signed by the donor, or (ii) acknowledged as such in a writing signed by the donee.

3. **Transfers to Minors.** Minors do not have the legal capacity to manage property. There are three options available to parents of minors for property management: guardianship, custodianship, and trusteeship. Custodianships and trusteeships may be created only during the lifetime of the creator or by will. A guardian or conservator will be appointed by the court if property is left to a minor child and the parent dies intestate.

C. BARS TO SUCCESSION

1. Misconduct.

a. Killing decedent--

***In re* Estate of Mahoney,** 220 A.2d 475 (Vt. 1966).

Facts. The decedent, Howard Mahoney, died intestate after being shot to death by his wife, Charlotte Mahoney (P), who was convicted of manslaughter and sentenced to prison. The decedent was survived only by P and his parents. The trial court entered a judgment decreeing the residue of the decedent's estate to his parents in equal shares. P appeals.

Issue. Can a widow convicted of manslaughter for the death of her husband inherit from his estate?

Held. Yes. Judgment reversed.

- ◆ There are three separate lines of cases dealing with this issue: (i) some states hold that legal title passes to the slayer and may be retained in spite of the crime; (ii) some states hold that legal title does not pass to the slayer because of the principle that no one should be permitted to profit by his own wrong; and (iii) some states hold that legal title passes to the slayer but equity holds him to be a constructive trustee for the heirs or next of kin of the decedent.

- ◆ We adopt the third line of cases. However, in this case, the trial court did not decree the estate to the widow and then make her a constructive trustee of the estate for the benefit of the parents; rather, the court below decreed the estate directly to the parents. We reverse. The trial court was bound to follow the statutes of descent and distribution and decree the estate to the widow.

- ◆ Further, jurisdiction to impose a constructive trust rests with the chancery court, not the probate court. Accordingly, we remand this case so that application may be made to the chancery court for purposes of imposing a constructive trust and for determination of whether the death of the husband was voluntary manslaughter or involuntary manslaughter. If no such application is made, then the probate court shall assign to the widow the interest in the estate of her deceased husband.

---

b. **Adultery.** In a few states, a spouse is disqualified from dower, inheritance, or an elective share if the spouse abandoned the decedent and committed adultery.

   c. **Desertion.** States may disqualify a parent as an heir if the parent has failed or refused to support the child or has abandoned the child during his minority.

2. **Transfer of Interest in Decedent's Estate.** A person may be barred from succeeding to a decedent's estate because he has released, transferred, or disclaimed his interest.

   a. **Release of expectancy.** A child's release to his parent during the parent's lifetime is binding if given for fair consideration.

   b. **Transfer of expectancy.** An expectancy is merely the possibility of inheriting property and, as such, it cannot be transferred, although a purported transfer of an expectancy for consideration may be enforceable in equity.

   c. **Disclaimer.** It has always been held that a beneficiary can disclaim any testamentary gift. If a beneficiary makes a valid disclaimer, the disclaimed interest passes as though the disclaimant predeceased the testator. If a person disclaims, and the disclaimer is not "qualified," *i.e.,* the person has not made an irrevocable and unqualified refusal of an interest in property under Internal Revenue Code section 2518 procedures, gift tax liability results. The disclaimer must be made within nine months after the interest is created or after the donee reaches age 21, whichever is later.

      1) **Disclaimer upheld--**

Troy v. Hart, 697 A.2d 113 (Md. 1996), *cert. denied*, 700 A.2d 1215 (Md. 1997).

Facts. Paul Lettich, a resident of Stella Maris Hospice ("Stella Maris"), was receiving Medicare and Medicaid benefits when his sister died intestate. One of Lettich's two surviving sisters, Hart (D), was appointed personal representative of her deceased sister's estate, and although D was aware Lettich was represented by Troy (P), D visited Lettich and helped him execute a disclaimer to his $100,000 share of the deceased sister's estate. D did not advise Lettich of the effect of the disclaimer on his Medicaid status and she divided the $100,000 with their other sister. P was notified of the renunciation the following month. Counsel for Lettich filed a petition to rescind the disclaimer and remove D as personal representative of the deceased sister's estate. One day before the deadline to respond to the petition, D's attorney visited Lettich and asked him to execute a motion to strike the petition. A social worker intervened and suggested P be consulted. Lettich died shortly thereafter. The court denied P's petition. P appealed. D's motion for judgment with respect to P's request to have her removed was granted; P's petition to rescind was dismissed. P appeals.

Issue. May a Medicaid recipient disclaim an inheritance?

Held. Yes. Judgment affirmed.

- ♦ Maryland law requires that once an individual is eligible for and receiving Medicaid benefits, he must notify the Department of Social Services ("DSS") within 10 working days of changes affecting eligibility.

- ♦ Lettich failed to notify DSS of his inheritance and thereby violated applicable Medicaid law and deprived both the state and federal governments of an opportunity to reevaluate his eligibility.

- ♦ A New York court has found in similar circumstances that renunciation of an intestate share is irreconcilable with the concept that public aid is limited and should be reserved for those who have a legitimate need, that a renunciation is essentially equal to a transfer, and should be penalized in the same manner. We adopt the reasoning of the New York court here.

- ♦ If a renunciation would cause a benefits recipient to be disqualified, the renunciation should be treated as a transfer and incur the same penalty that a transfer prior to eligibility would incur. The recipient should be liable for any payments incorrectly paid by the state in consequence of the renunciation.

- ♦ While Lettich's disclaimer is valid, his surviving sisters should take subject to any claims the state may have against Lettich's estate for any payments improperly made as a result of Lettich's failure to notify DSS of his acquisition of property.

- ♦ A constructive trust is applied where circumstances render it inequitable for the party holding title to retain it, as here.

––––––––––––––

III. WILLS: CAPACITY AND CONTESTS

A. MENTAL CAPACITY

1. **Test of Mental Capacity.** The decedent must know: (i) the nature and extent of her property; (ii) the persons who are the natural objects of her bounty; (iii) the disposition she is making; and (iv) how these elements relate in planning for the disposition of her property.

   a. **Isolated acts--**

In re Estate of Wright, 60 P.2d 434 (Cal. 1936).

Facts. Wright (T) died 16 months after executing a will that devised a house, personal belongings, and money to his friend, Charlotte Hindmarch, who was named as the executrix. T also devised a house to his daughter, his interest in an estate to his granddaughter, and one dollar to his grandson and several other people. T's daughter contested the will. During the proceeding, testimony established that Mrs. Thomas, a notary public who had known T for many years, had prepared T's will. Mrs. Thomas and both witnesses to the will testified that T was of unsound mind when he executed the will. Other acquaintances and relatives also testified that T was not of sound mind, based on T's peculiarities, his drinking, a head injury he once suffered, a serious operation he had several years before his death, and isolated idiosyncratic acts. The petition for admission of the will to probate was denied on the ground of testamentary incapacity. The executrix appeals.

Issue. Is evidence of a testator's isolated peculiar acts and unusual lifestyle, without evidence of insanity, hallucinations, or delusions, sufficient to deny probate of his will?

Held. No. Judgment reversed.

♦ In a will contest, sanity is presumed, and the one contesting the will has the burden of proving that the testator was of unsound mind when he executed his will.

♦ The drawer of a will and the subscribing witnesses have a duty to be satisfied of the testator's sanity before giving their stamp of approval and verity to the will's execution. If they later testify that the testator was of unsound mind, their testimony will be subject to close scrutiny and suspicion.

♦ Isolated acts, idiosyncrasies, moral or mental irregularities, or departures from the norm cannot destroy testamentary capacity unless they directly influenced the testamentary act. In this case, there was no medical testimony and no evidence of settled insanity, hallucinations, or delusions.

- No testimony was offered to rebut T's ability to transact business or care for himself except for a few cases of illness brought about by natural causes, excesses, or accident. T knew the extent of his property and appreciated his relations and obligations to others. He went alone to have his will prepared with a list of beneficiaries that he had prepared himself.

---

2. **Why Require Mental Capacity?** Mental capacity is required for the protection of society and for the protection of the decedent's family and the decedent herself.

3. **Insane Delusion.** An insane delusion is an extreme misconception of reality to which the testator adheres against all proof to the contrary.

   a. **Insane delusions about men--**

In re **Strittmater,** 53 A.2d 205 (N.J. 1947).

Facts. Strittmater (T) never married. She lived with her parents until their death and was devoted to them and they to her. Four years after their death, she wrote that her father was "a corrupt, vicious, and unintelligent savage," typical of the majority of his sex, and on a photograph of her mother, she inscribed, "moronic she-devil." T's dealings with her attorney, over a period of years, were normal. T became a member of the National Women's Party and volunteered one day a week for at least two years. In her will, she left her estate to the party, as had been her expressed intention. T died one month after her will was executed. The will was admitted to probate. Two cousins challenged the will, alleging it was a product of T's insanity. A lower court set aside the will. That court's decree is appealed.

Issue. May a will that was executed by a person with insane delusions about men be admitted to probate?

Held. No. Decree affirmed.

- T's female physician opined T suffered from a split personality.

- T had been a member of the party for 11 years when she wrote: "It remains for feminist organizations like [the party] to make exposure of women's 'protectors' and 'lovers' for what their vicious and contemptible selves are."

- It was T's paranoiac condition, especially her insane delusions about the male, that led her to leave her estate to the party. Probate should be set aside.

---

b. Insane delusion resulting from irrational belief in nonexistent facts--

---

In re **Honigman,** 168 N.E.2d 676 (N.Y. 1960).

Facts. Prior to his death, the decedent, Frank Honigman, told friends and strangers alike that he believed his wife was unfaithful. This suspicion became an obsession, although he was normal and rational in other respects. The decedent, a man of 70 who had undergone a number of operations, once commented that he was sick in the head and that he knew something was wrong with him. The decedent instructed his attorney to prepare a will cutting off his wife from any of his estate, leaving her life use of her minimum statutory share, with directions to pay the principal upon her death to his surviving brothers or sisters and to the descendants of any predeceased brother or sister, per stirpes. At the trial, the proponents of the will adduced evidence which, they argued, showed a reasonable basis for the decedent's belief. This included an anniversary card sent by a Mr. Krause to the decedent's wife, a letter, evidence that whenever the phone rang the decedent's wife would answer it, and evidence that Mr. Krause came over to the decedent's house one night while the decedent was out. When the will was offered for probate, the decedent's widow (P) filed objections. A trial was conducted on the issue of whether the deceased was of sound mind and memory at the time he signed the will. The jury answered in the negative. The appellate court reversed. This appeal followed.

Issue. If a person believes facts that are against all evidence and probability and conducts himself, however logically, upon the assumption of their existence in making his will, does he suffer from an insane delusion so as to defeat testamentary capacity?

Held. Yes. Judgment reversed and a new trial ordered.

- The general rule is that if a person persistently believes supposed facts that have no real existence except in his perverted imagination and against all evidence and probability, and conducts himself, however logically, upon the assumption of their existence, he is, so far as they are concerned, under a morbid delusion. Such a person is essentially mad or insane on those subjects.

- Here, the issue of the decedent's sanity was an issue for the jury to resolve. There was sufficient evidence to justify placing this issue before the jury: the decedent's repeated suspicions of P's unfaithfulness; his belief of P's misbehaving by hiding male callers under her bed and by hauling men from the street up to her bedroom by the use of sheets; and so forth.

- The proponents argue that even if the decedent was laboring under a delusion, other reasons support the validity of the will. We disagree. A will is invalid if its dispository provisions might have been caused or affected by the delusion.

- Finally, we hold that the Dead Man's Statute—which excludes the testimony of a witness concerning a personal communication between the witness and the deceased—was misconstrued to permit the testimony of P when an objection to her testimony had been properly raised.

Dissent. The evidence adduced utterly failed to prove that the testator was suffering from an insane delusion or lacked testamentary capacity. Much of the evidence was improperly admitted, as the court itself notes, by reason of the Dead Man's Statute.

B. UNDUE INFLUENCE

A will or a gift in a will may be set aside if it was the result of undue influence—mental coercion that destroyed the testator's free will and forced him to embody someone else's intention in his will in place of his own.

1. **Subjective Test.** The test of whether a testator has been subjected to undue influence is a subjective one, measured at the time of execution of the will. The evidence must establish: (i) that undue influence was exerted on the testator; (ii) that the effect of the influence must have been to overpower the mind and will of the testator; and (iii) that the influence must have produced a will or a gift in the will that expresses the intent not of the testator but of the one exerting the influence, and that would not have been made but for the influence.

2. **Requirement of Proof Showing Substitution of a Plan of Testamentary Disposition--**

Lipper v. Weslow, 369 S.W.2d 698 (Tex. 1963).

Facts. Mrs. Sophie Block (T) executed a will written by her son, Frank Lipper, a lawyer, 22 days before she died. Lipper bore malice against his deceased half-brother, who was excluded from the will. This resulted in Lipper receiving a larger share under the will than he otherwise would have received. Lipper lived next door to T and had a key to her home. After signing the will, T told one witness that she was leaving her estate to her son and daughter and that her other son, Julian A. Weslow, and his children would be excluded because they never showed any attention to her. The will provided a lengthy explanation as to why Julian was excluded from the will largely due to the "unfriendly and distant attitude" T felt had been accorded to her. The children of Julian Weslow (Ps) contest the will, charging Frank Lipper and Irene Lipper Dover (Ds) with undue influence. At trial, a jury found that T's will was procured by undue influence. Ds appeal, contending that there is no evidence to support this finding.

Issue. Must a person contesting a will on the basis of undue influence supply proof of the substitution of the plan of testamentary disposition by another as the will of the testatrix?

Held. Yes. Judgment reversed and rendered for Ds.

♦   The contestants have established a confidential relationship, the opportunity, and perhaps a motive for undue influence. However, they must go forward and prove in some fashion that the will as written resulted from D's substituting his mind and will for that of T. Proof of vital facts of undue influence must be provided: the substitution of a plan of testamentary disposition by another as the will of T.

♦ Here, the evidence shows that T was of sound mind, of strong will, and in excellent physical condition. A person of sound mind has the legal right to dispose of her property as she wishes, with the burden on those attacking the disposition to prove that it was the product of undue influence. T had a legal right to do what she did whether we think she was justified or not. We conclude that there was no evidence of probative force to support the verdict of the jury.

---

3. Undue Influence Arising out of Attorney-Client Relationship--

---

***In re* Will of Moses,** 227 So. 2d 829 (Miss. 1969).

Facts. Fannie Taylor Moses (T), during her second marriage, became friends with Clarence Holland, an attorney. After the death of T's third husband, Holland became T's lover, as well as her attorney. Before her death, T suffered from heart trouble, had a breast removed because of cancer, and became an alcoholic. Three years prior to her death, she made a will devising virtually all of her property to Holland. This will was drafted by a lawyer who had no connection with Clarence Holland, nor did Holland know about the will. T's eldest sister (P) attacked the will on the ground of undue influence. The trial court found for P. Holland appeals.

Issue. Does a presumption of undue influence exist where a sexual relationship between attorney and client coexists with the attorney-client relationship?

Held. Yes. Judgment affirmed.

♦ It is argued that even if Holland, T's attorney, occupied a fiduciary relationship on the date of execution of the will, the presumption of undue influence is overcome since T had the independent advice and counsel of an attorney. We disagree. The evidence here shows that the attorney who drafted the will was little more than a scrivener, and that there was no meaningful independent advice or counsel touching upon the area in question.

♦ Here, the intimate nature of this relationship is relevant to the question of undue influence to the extent that its existence warranted an inference of undue influence, extending and augmenting that which flowed from the attorney-client relationship. This is particularly true when it is considered that Holland will personally benefit from the will as drafted.

Dissent. There is not one iota of evidence in the record that Holland even knew of the will, much less that he participated in the preparation or execution of it. The evidence is to the contrary. T prepared her will on the advice of independent counsel whose sole purpose was to advise her and prepare the will exactly as she wanted it.

---

4. **Undue Influence a Question of Fact Where Testator Is Easily Swayed.** Under the facts in *In re Kaufmann's Will*, 247 N.Y.S.2d 664 (1964), *aff'd,* 205 N.E.2d 864 (N.Y. 1965), the decedent, Robert Kaufmann, a millionaire by inheritance, lived with Walter Weiss for some eight years, during which time Robert, in successive wills, increased Walter's share of his estate. Upon Robert's death, his brother Joel sued to have the final will, drafted in 1958, set aside on the ground of undue influence. In his deposition, Walter denied that a homosexual relationship existed between the two men. After two jury trials, both finding undue influence, the court of appeals affirmed, stating that "where, as here, the record indicates that testator was pliable and easily taken advantage of, that there was a long and detailed history of dominance and subservience between them, that testator relied exclusively upon proponent's knowledge . . . and proponent is willed virtually the entire estate, we consider that a question of fact was presented concerning whether [there had been undue influence]."

5. **No-Contest Clauses.** A no-contest clause in a will provides that any person who contests the will shall forfeit all interests he otherwise would have received under that will. If a beneficiary contesting the will is successful, the no-contest clause fails with the will. In most states and under the UPC, a beneficiary who unsuccessfully contests the will does not forfeit the legacy if the court finds that the beneficiary challenged the will in *good faith* and on the basis of *probable cause*. A minority view gives full effect to no-contest clauses even if the losing contestant had probable cause for challenging the will. A challenge based on an action brought to construe the will, on jurisdictional grounds, or on the appointment of an executor, or to the accounting made by that person, is not considered a contest to the will that would result in a forfeiture under a no-contest clause.

C. FRAUD

1. **Definition.** Fraud consists of (i) false statements of material facts, (ii) known to be false by the party making the statements, (iii) made with the intention of deceiving the testator, (iv) which actually deceive the testator, and (v) which cause the testator to act in reliance on the false statements.

   a. **Fraud in the execution.** This type of fraud (also known as fraud in the factum) includes cases where the testator was tricked into signing a document not knowing it to be a will, and cases where one will is substituted for another.

   b.   **Fraud in the inducement.** This type of fraud includes those cases where the testator is fraudulently induced into making the will (*e.g.,* in return for a false promise of care).

D. DURESS

   1.   **Constructive Trust Imposed Where Testator Prevented from Executing Will--**

Latham v. Father Divine, 85 N.E.2d 168 (N.Y. 1949).

Facts. The complaint brought by Ps (first cousins of the decedent) alleged the following facts: The will of Mary Sheldon Lyon (T) gave almost her whole estate to Father Divine, leader of a religious cult (D), two corporate defendants (Ds), and to Patience Budd (D), one of Father Divine's active followers. After making the will, T expressed a desire to revoke the will and to execute a new will by which Ps would receive a substantial portion of the estate. T, shortly before her death, had attorneys draft a new will for her with Ps receiving a substantial sum. However before T could execute this will, Ds, by undue influence and physical force, prevented T from executing the will. The complaint brought by Ps alleged that Ds conspired to kill, and did kill, T by means of a surgical operation performed by a doctor engaged by Ds without the consent or knowledge of any relatives of T. The will that T did sign was probated under a compromise agreement in a proceeding in which Ps were not parties. The trial court upheld the complaint but the appellate court dismissed it on grounds of insufficiency. Ps appeal.

Issue. When an heir or devisee in a will prevents the testator from providing for one for whom she would have provided but for the interference of the heir or devisee, will that heir or devisee be deemed a trustee of the property received by him to the extent that the defrauded party would have received had not the deceased been interfered with?

Held. Yes. Judgment of the appellate court reversed.

♦   The general rule is that where an heir or devisee in a will prevents the testator from providing for one for whom she would have provided but for the interference of the heir or devisee, that heir or devisee will be deemed a trustee, by operation of law, of the property, real or personal, received by him from the testator's estate, to the amount or extent that the defrauded party would have received had not the intention of the deceased been interfered with.

♦   This is not a proceeding to probate the will nor is it an attempt to accomplish a revocation of the earlier will. The complaint alleges that by force and fraud Ds kept T from making a will in favor of Ps. We cannot say as a matter of law that no constructive trust can arise therefrom.

♦   A constructive trust will be erected whenever necessary to satisfy the ends of justice. Here, the probated will has full effect, but equity, in order to defeat the fraud, raises a trust in favor of those intended to be benefitted by the testator and compels the legatee to turn over the gift to them.

Comment. Tortious interference with an expectancy is another theory that can be used to rectify fraud or undue influence. [Restatement (Second) of Torts §774B (1979)] The plaintiff must prove the interference involved conduct tortious in and of itself, *e.g.*, fraud, duress, undue influence.

———————————————

IV. WILLS: FORMALITIES AND FORMS

A. EXECUTION OF WILLS

1. **Attested Wills.** The standard form of a will is one that is signed by the testator and witnessed by two witnesses pursuant to a formal attestation procedure.

   a. **Requirements of due execution.** For a will to be valid and admissible to probate, the testator must meet the formal requirements of due execution imposed by statutes of the appropriate state. These requirements vary from state to state, and generally include requiring the testator to sign at the end of the will and in the presence of all attesting witnesses. The testator might also be required to publish the will, *i.e.,* declare to the witnesses that the instrument is her will.

   b. **Requirement that both witnesses be present.** *In re Groffman*, 1 W.L.R. 733 (1969), the court refused to admit a will to probate because the two witnesses were not present together when Groffman, the testator, signed his will or acknowledged his signature. All three of the men were together in the same room of a house, but Groffman and the first witness went to an adjacent room where the first witness signed Groffman's will. When the first witness returned, the second witness went to the other room to sign the will. Even though the witnesses and the testator were together in the same house and Groffman's intent was clear, the court denied probate.

   c. **A narrow exception to rules of execution--**

Stevens v. Casdorph, 508 S.E.2d 610 (W. Va. 1998).

Facts. The Casdorphs (Ds) took Miller to the bank to execute his will. At the bank, Miller asked a notary to witness the execution, which she did. After Miller signed the will, the notary took the will to two other bank employees to witness the signature. Miller was not with her when the witnesses signed the will, they had not seen Miller sign, and they had not seen each other sign. Upon Miller's death, Paul Casdorph, Miller's nephew, was named executor, and the Casdorphs were left the bulk of the estate. The Stevenses (Ps), who as nieces would share in an intestate estate, filed suit to set aside the will because it was not properly executed. All parties moved for summary judgment. The court granted Ds' motion for summary judgment, and Ps appeal.

Issue. For a will to be properly executed, must the testator sign or acknowledge his will in the presence of two witnesses, present at the same time, and must the witnesses sign the will or acknowledge their signatures in the presence of each other and the testator?

Held. Yes. Judgment reversed.

♦ Although the law favors testacy over intestacy, the relevant statute requires that the testator sign or acknowledge his will in the presence of two witnesses, present at the same time, and that the witnesses sign the will or acknowledge their signatures in the presence of each other and the testator.

♦ Ds contend that there was substantial compliance with the statute because everyone involved with the will knew what was going on. Furthermore, the trial court found that there was no evidence of fraud, coercion, or undue influence. However, mere intent by a testator to execute a will is insufficient.

♦ This court has allowed only a narrow exception to the rules of execution. If a witness acknowledges his signature on a will in the physical presence of the other witness and the testator, then the will is properly witnessed. Here, none of the parties signed or acknowledged their signatures in the presence of each other.

Dissent. The majority worships form over substance, and its conclusion is harsh and inequitable.

—————————————

　　d.　**Competency of witnesses.** Witnesses must be competent. This generally means that at the time the will is executed the witness must be mature enough and of sufficient mental capacity to understand and appreciate the nature of the act he is witnessing and to be able to testify in court should this be necessary.

　　　　1)　**Interested witnesses.** At common law, if an attesting witness was also a beneficiary of a will, the witness-beneficiary was not a competent witness and the will was denied probate. Today, however, most jurisdictions have interested witness statutes, which provide that if an attesting witness is also a beneficiary, the gift to the witness is void but the witness is a competent witness and the will may be probated.

　　　　2)　**Requirement of disinterestedness--**

Estate of Parsons, 163 Cal. Rptr. 70 (1980).

Facts. Three persons signed the will of the decedent, Geneve Parsons (T): Evelyn Nielson, Marie Gower (D), and Bob Warda, a notary public. Two of them, Nielson and Gower, were named in the will as beneficiaries. After T's death, her will was admitted to probate. Nielson then filed a disclaimer of her bequest in the will. Thereafter, distant relatives of T (Ps) claimed an interest in the estate on the ground that the devise to Gower was invalid. The trial court rejected that argument. Ps appeal.

Issues.

(i)   Is a subscribing witness to a will who is named in the will as a beneficiary a disinterested subscribing witness as required by statute?

(ii)   Is a subsequent disclaimer effective to transform an interested witness into a "disinterested" one?

Held. (i) No. (ii) No. Judgment reversed.

♦   Probate Code section 51 provides that a gift to a subscribing witness is void unless there are two other disinterested witnesses to the will. Ps contend that a subsequent disclaimer is ineffective to transform an interested witness into a disinterested one. They assert that because there was only one disinterested witness at the time of attestation, the devise to D is void by operation of law. D, however, points to language in Probate Code section 190.6 that states "in every case, the disclaimer shall relate back for all purposes to the date of creation of the interest."

♦   At common law a party to an action, or one who had a direct interest in its outcome, was not competent to testify in court because it was thought that an interested witness would be tempted to perjure himself in favor of his interest. If any one of the requisite number of attesting witnesses was also a beneficiary, then the entire will would fail. Parliament, in 1752, enacted a statute that saved the will by providing that the interest of an attesting witness was void; under such legislation, the competence of a witness to testify is restored by invalidating his gift. The majority of jurisdictions have similar statutes; section 51 falls into this category.

♦   The essential function of a subscribing witness is performed when the will is executed. We believe section 51 looks in its operation solely to that time. It operates to insure that at least two of the subscribing witnesses are disinterested.

♦   Because we hold that section 51 looks solely to the time of execution and attestation of the will, it follows that a subsequent disclaimer will be ineffective to transform an interested witness into a disinterested one within the meaning of that section. D's reliance on section 190.6 is misplaced—that section serves to equalize the tax consequences of disclaimers as between heirs at law and testamentary beneficiaries.

---

e.   **Recommended method of executing a will.** A decedent might not die in the jurisdiction where the will was executed, thus giving rise to potential conflict of laws issues. The validity of the will in disposing personal property is determined according to the laws of the decedent's domicile at death. The validity of the will in disposing real property is determined according to the laws of the state where that property is located. Hence, the will should be executed so that it will be admitted to probate in all jurisdictions involved.

f.   **Self-proving affidavit.** The great majority of states have adopted a self-proving affidavit procedure in which the testator and the witnesses, after executing the will, execute before a notary public an affidavit reciting that all of the requisites for due execution have been complied with. This allows the will to be probated if the witnesses are dead, cannot be located, or have moved far away.

g.   **Safeguarding a will.** An attorney's retention of a client's will may have the appearance of soliciting business, which is an unethical practice. Many states have statutes permitting deposit of wills with the clerk of the probate court.

h.   **Mistake in execution of a will--**

In re **Pavlinko's Estate,** 148 A.2d 528 (Pa. 1959).

Facts. The decedent, Vasil Pavlinko (T), by mistake signed the will of his wife, Hellen, and Hellen by mistake signed the will of her husband, T. The drafting attorney and his secretary signed as witnesses. A brother of Hellen, who was the residuary legatee of both wills, offered for probate as T's will the will that purported to be the will of Hellen Pavlinko, but which was signed by her husband. The trial court refused to probate the will. This appeal followed.

Issue. Will a court reform a will to allow probate when there is a mistake in execution of the will in that one party mistakenly signs the will of another?

Held. No. Judgment affirmed.

♦   The Wills Act provides in clear language that every will shall be in writing and shall be signed by the testator at the end thereof. The court below correctly held that the paper that recited that it was the will of Hellen Pavlinko could not be probated as the will of T and was a nullity.

♦   To decide in favor of the residuary legatee, almost the entire will would have to be rewritten. Here, the paper signed was not T's will. He had executed no will and there was nothing to be reformed. He therefore died intestate and his property descends as at law. Were we to rewrite wills or make exceptions to the clear provisions of the Wills Act, the Act would become meaningless and would encourage fraudulent claims.

Dissent. The majority does not make a serious effort to effectuate the intent of the testator. The fact that some of the provisions in the will cannot be executed does not strike down the residuary clause, which is meaningful and stands independently. Some of the provisions are not effective, but their ineffectuality in no way bars the legality and validity of the residuary clause, which is complete in itself.

---

i. Substitution of names to reform will--

In re **Snide,** 418 N.E.2d 656 (N.Y. 1981).

Facts. At an execution of mutual wills, Harvey and Rose Snide signed the will intended for the other by mistake. The wills were presented to the parties in envelopes with their names on them, and the other's will was in the envelope each received. No one looked at the beginning pages. Except for the differences in the names of the donors and beneficiaries, the wills were identical. When Harvey died, Rose offered the will he signed for probate. Their two older children executed waivers and consented to the admission. Their minor child was represented by a guardian ad litem who refused to consent. If the estate were to pass by intestacy, the minor would receive a present share of the estate. Otherwise, the entire estate would pass to Rose. The surrogate allowed the will to be reformed by substituting "Harvey" wherever "Rose" appeared and "Rose" wherever "Harvey" appeared. The will was admitted, but the appellate division reversed. Rose appeals.

Issue. May a will that was executed in compliance with the required formalities be admitted to probate if the decedent and his wife, intending to execute mutual wills, each mistakenly executed the will intended for the other?

Held. Yes. Judgment reversed.

- ♦ Although the decedent did not intend to execute the document that he actually signed, we reject the formal view that intent attaches to the document prepared rather than to the testamentary scheme reflected in the document. If a carbon copy had been presented and signed, the intent would not be frustrated. Here, except for the names of the donors and beneficiaries, the dispositive provisions in both documents were the same.

- ♦ The instrument was genuine, and it was properly executed. What was intended is clear, and what occurred is obvious.

Dissent. I would adhere to precedents and affirm the order of the appellate division.

---

j. Self-proved wills--

In re **Will of Ranney,** 589 A.2d 1339 (N.J. 1991).

Facts. Russell Ranney (T) executed a four-page will before a notary and two witnesses. T acknowledged that the instrument was his will and he wanted the witnesses to act as witnesses. T signed the will on the unnumbered fourth page, and the witnesses simultaneously signed a self-proving affidavit on the fifth page. All parties believed they were complying with statutory attestation requirements. All signatures were notarized and the fifth page was stapled to the fourth. The attestation clause refers to the execution of the will in the past tense and states that each witness "signed the Will as witnesses." Upon T's death, the will was admitted to probate. T's wife contested, claiming that the will failed to comply literally with the statutory formalities. The superior court ruled that the will did not contain the signatures of two witnesses. The appellate division reversed and found the affidavit to be a part of the will, and, therefore, the witnesses had signed. The supreme court granted T's wife's petition for certification.

Issue. Should an instrument purporting to be a last will and testament that includes the signature of two witnesses on an attached self-proving affidavit, but not on the will itself, be admitted to probate?

Held. Yes. Judgment affirmed.

- We do not agree with the appellate division that a will containing witnesses' signatures only on a self-proving affidavit literally complies with attestation requirements. The court's rationale was that an affidavit and an attestation clause are sufficiently similar to justify the conclusion that signatures on an affidavit, like signatures on the attestation clause, satisfy the requirement that the signatures be on the will. This conclusion fails to consider the basic differences between a subsequently-executed, self-proving affidavit and an attestation clause.

- Attestation clauses (i) provide "prima facie evidence" that the will was signed by the testator in the presence of witnesses; (ii) permit probate when a witness forgets the circumstances of execution or dies before the testator; and (iii) express the present intent of the attestant to act as witness.

- Self-proving affidavits are sworn statements that the will has been executed and has already been witnessed. The affidavit performs all of the functions of the attestation clause and permits probate without requiring either witness to appear.

- Here, affiants, intending to act as witnesses, signed the affidavit immediately after witnessing T's execution of the will.

- Nothing in statutory language or history suggests that the legislature contemplated a subsequently executed affidavit as a substitute for the attestation clause. The legislature did indicate its intention that subsequently executed, self-proving affidavits be used solely in conjunction with duly executed wills. In the instant case, the affidavit does not comply with statutory requirements.

- In limited circumstances, however, a will that "substantially complies" with statutory requirements may be admitted to probate. Other states, scholars, and treatises have determined that "substantial compliance better serves the goals of statutory formalities by permitting probate of formally defective wills that nevertheless represent the intent of the testator."

♦ Formalities in execution of wills (i) are meant to insure that the instrument reflects the testator's uncoerced intent; (ii) perform the function of providing uniformity in the organization, language, and content of a will; and (iii) provide a ritual that underscores the seriousness of the occasion. These purposes are often frustrated when rigid insistence on literal compliance invalidates a will that is the deliberate and voluntary act of the testator.

♦ The variation of the UPC adopted by the state legislature in 1977 minimizes the formalities of execution: (i) witnesses are not required to sign in the presence of the testator and each other; (ii) a beneficiary who acts as a witness is no longer prevented from taking; and (iii) unwitnessed holographic wills may be admitted to probate. Thus, we believe the legislature did not intend that a will should be denied probate because the witnesses signed in the wrong place.

♦ Because an affidavit serves a unique function, we are reluctant to permit the signatures on an affidavit to both validate the signatures on the will and to render the will self-proving. However, if the witnesses, with the intent to attest, sign a self-proving affidavit, but do not sign the will or an attestation clause, clear and convincing evidence of their intent should be adduced to establish substantial compliance with the statute.

k. No attesting witnesses--

In re Estate of Hall, 51 P.3d 1134 (Mont. 2002).

Facts. Jim Hall died, leaving a wife, Betty, and two daughters. Jim's original will had been executed in 1984. Thirteen years later, the Halls' attorney sent them a draft of a joint will. Later, at a meeting with the attorney, the will was discussed and changes were made. The Halls were prepared to execute the joint will when the final version came. Jim asked if the draft will could stand until the new one was signed. The attorney said the draft would be valid if it were signed and notarized. There were no witnesses available, but the will was signed and the attorney notarized it. When the couple arrived home, Jim told Betty to tear up the original will, which she did. After Jim's death, Betty applied to informally probate the draft joint will. Sandra, a daughter, objected. After a hearing, the joint will was admitted to probate. Sandra appeals.

Issue. If no witnesses are present at the execution of a will, may the document be treated as if it had been properly executed if the proponent of the document establishes that the decedent intended the document to constitute his will?

Held. Yes. Judgment affirmed.

- For a will to be valid, two people typically must witness the testator signing the will and then sign it themselves.

- In contested cases, the proponent of a will must establish that the testator duly executed the will. However, if a will proponent establishes by clear and convincing evidence that the decedent intended the document to be his last will, the document may be treated as if it had been properly executed. The Montana legislature has provided this means of validating a will.

- Here, the evidence indicates that the decedent intended the draft to stand as his will. He executed the will, revoked all previous wills, and directed his wife to destroy the original will.

---

2. **Holographic Wills.** A holographic will is handwritten and signed by the testator; attesting witnesses are not required. About half of the states permit holographic wills. Under the UPC, a holographic will is valid if the signature and the material provisions are in the handwriting of the testator even if not witnessed.

   a. **Informal will--**

Kimmel's Estate, 123 A. 405 (Pa. 1924).

Facts. A letter mailed by the decedent, Kimmel (T), to two of his children, who were named as beneficiaries therein, was admitted to probate. T died the afternoon of the day he wrote the letter. One of T's heirs objected to the admission and now appeals.

Issues.

(i) May an informal letter be testamentary in character?

(ii) Is the signature "Father" sufficient to comply with the Wills Act?

Held. (i) Yes. (ii) Yes. Decree affirmed and appeal dismissed.

- Where a testator's purpose was to make a posthumous gift, we have held deeds, letters, powers of attorney, and an informal letter of requests as wills.

- T's contingency here, "if enny thing hapens," was still existing when he died suddenly, and the question of testamentary intent is one of law for the courts.

- T's words make it difficult to determine that he meant anything other than a testamentary gift, and his act of sending the letter to the persons for whom the gift was intended gives further support to that determination.

♦ The signature "Father" was intended as a complete signature. It was the method employed by T in signing all such letters and was mailed by T as a finished document.

---

b. **Testamentary provisions not in handwriting of testator.** *In re Estate of Johnson*, 630 P.2d 1039 (Ariz. 1981), involved a will that was on a printed will form available in various office supply stores. It contained certain printed provisions followed by blanks where he could insert any provisions he might desire. The court held that the will could not be admitted to probate because the only words that established the decedent's requisite testamentary intent were in the printed portion of the form.

c. **Holographic codicil--**

In re **Estate of Kuralt,** 15 P.3d 931 (Mont. 2000).

Facts. Charles Kuralt, famous for his "On the Road" series, had a long-term romance with Pat Shannon after meeting her for one of the "On the Road" stories. Because he was married, he kept his relationship with Shannon secret. Over the next 30 years, Kuralt spoke to Shannon often and provided financial support, including a vacation home in Ireland. He also had a close, personal relationship with Shannon's children. In 1985, Shannon moved to a cabin that she and Kuralt had built for them on 20 acres in Montana. Kuralt later purchased land to the north and south of the Montana property, resulting in a 90-acre parcel. In 1989, Kuralt executed a holographic will bequeathing all of the Montana property, including furnishings and personal belongings, to Shannon and sent a copy to her. In 1994, he executed a formal will, making his wife and children the beneficiaries, but he did not specifically mention any real property. Kuralt deeded the original 20 acres with the cabin to Shannon in 1997, and he disguised the transaction as a sale, supplying the "purchase price" to Shannon before the transfer. After the new deed was filed, Shannon sent Kuralt a blank buy-sell form so the remaining property could be conveyed in the same way. This transfer was to take place at the cabin in four months, but Kuralt was hospitalized before the two could meet. Two weeks before his death in 1997, Kuralt wrote a letter to Shannon, assuring her that she would inherit the Montana property. Kuralt failed, however, to contact an attorney to make those arrangements. Upon Kuralt's death, Shannon sought to probate the 1997 letter as a valid holographic codicil to Kuralt's will. The estate opposed Shannon's petition, and the district court granted partial summary judgment for the estate. This court reversed and remanded to resolve disputed issues of material fact. After a hearing, the district court held that the 1997 letter was a valid codicil and entered judgment for Shannon. The estate appeals.

Issue. May a letter express a present testamentary intent to transfer property so that it may be admitted to probate as a holographic will or codicil?

Held. Yes. Judgment affirmed.

◆   Montana courts are guided by the principle of honoring the intent of the testator. In this case, Kuralt and Shannon enjoyed a long, close personal relationship. Kuralt also had a family-like relationship with Shannon's children and gave them significant financial support. Kuralt conveyed the 20-acre parcel of land in Montana to Shannon for no real consideration, and there was extrinsic evidence that he intended to transfer the remainder of the Montana property to her in a similar manner. However, his illness thwarted his plans.

◆   Kuralt died two weeks after writing the letter expressing his desire that Shannon inherit the remainder of the Montana property. Thus, it was written *in extremis*. Furthermore, he stressed his intention to make a posthumous disposition of the property by underling the word "inherit" in his letter.

B. REVOCATION OF WILLS

1. **Methods of Revocation.** A will may be revoked by one of three methods:

    a. **By operation of law.** If a testator gets married or divorced after executing a will, this change in status may revoke, by operation of law, all or part of the will.

    b. **By a later will or codicil.** In these instances, language that expressly revokes the prior will should be included. Alternatively, a later will may revoke a prior will if there are inconsistent provisions in the later will that impliedly revoke the earlier will.

    c. **By a physical act of destruction.** Generally, burning, tearing, or obliterating a material part of the will revokes it. Another person can do the tearing or burning if in the testator's presence and at his direction.

2. **Probate of Lost or Destroyed Wills.** In the absence of a statute, the fact that a will is lost, or is destroyed without the consent of the testator, does not prevent its probate, provided its contents are proved. Most states require proof of contents by testimony of persons who had knowledge of the contents of the will, as by having read the will or having heard it read. States that have statutes restricting the probate of lost or destroyed wills have narrowly construed them in order to permit probate.

3. **Revocation by Writing or Physical Act.** Under the UPC, a will or any part thereof is revoked (i) by a subsequent will that revokes the prior will or part of it expressly or by inconsistency; or (ii) by being burned, torn, canceled, obliterated, or destroyed, with the intent and for the purpose of revoking it by the testator or by another person in his presence and by his direction.

a. Presumption will destroyed--

Harrison v. Bird, 621 So. 2d 972 (Ala. 1993).

Facts. The decedent, Daisy Speer (T), executed a will naming Harrison (P) as the main beneficiary. T later called her attorney, who had the original will, to revoke the will. The attorney and his secretary tore up the will and wrote a letter to T confirming this and enclosing the torn pieces. He informed T she was without a will. Upon T's death, the letter was found, but not the torn pieces. Letters of administration were granted to Bird (D). P filed the copy of the revoked will for probate. The circuit court ruled that: (i) the will was not revoked because T was not present when her attorney destroyed the will; (ii) there could be no ratification of the destruction of the will as it had not been done pursuant to strict statutory requirements; and (iii) based on the fact that the pieces were not found after T's death, there was a presumption that T revoked the will herself. The court found that this presumption had not been rebutted by P and that the duplicate was not T's will. The court held that T's estate should be administered as an intestate estate. P appeals.

Issue. Was the evidence presented sufficient to rebut the presumption that T destroyed her will with the intent to revoke it?

Held. No. Judgment affirmed.

♦   Even though a duplicate exists that was not in T's possession, if T had possession of her will before her death, and the will is not found after her death, a presumption arises that T revoked her will and all duplicates.

♦   P argued that the facts that T's attorney destroyed the will outside of T's presence, T had possession of the pieces, and such pieces were not found, are not sufficient to invoke the presumption of revocation. This argument is without merit.

b. Attempted revocation by writing on paper upon which will is written--

Thompson v. Royall, 175 S.E. 748 (Va. 1934).

Facts. On September 4, 1932, the decedent, Mrs. Knoll (T), signed a will consisting of five sheets of legal paper. On September 19, 1932, at T's request, her attorney and her executor took the will and codicil to her home, where she told the attorney, in the presence of her executor and another, to destroy both. But instead of destroying them, she decided to retain them as memoranda. On the back of the manuscript cover, in the handwriting of her attorney, signed by T, there was written: "This will null and void and to be held only by (the executor) instead of being destroyed as a memorandum for another will if I desire to make same." The same notation was made on the back of the codicil, except that the name of the attorney was substituted for that of the executor. The jury found that the instruments were the last will and testament of T. From an order sustaining this verdict and probating the will, this appeal was taken.

Issue. Must written words used for revocation by cancellation of a will be so placed as to physically affect the written portion of the will and not merely the blank parts of the paper on which the will is written?

Held. Yes. Judgment affirmed.

♦ A will must be revoked as prescribed by statute, either by (i) some writing declaring an intention to revoke and executed in the same manner as a will or by (ii) cutting, tearing, burning, obliterating, canceling, or destroying the will with the intent to revoke.

♦ Here, the notations made on the back of the will are not wholly in T's handwriting, nor are her signatures attested by subscribing witnesses. Hence, under the statute they are ineffectual as "some writing declaring an intention to revoke."

♦ Nor are the words sufficient to revoke the will by cancellation by physical act. The statute contemplates marks or lines across the written parts of the instrument or a physical defacement or some mutilation of the writing itself with the intent to revoke. If written words are used for the purpose, they must be placed as to physically affect the written portion of the will, not merely the blank parts of the will on which the will is written. The attempted revocation is therefore ineffectual.

---

c. **Partial revocation by physical act.** Most statutes authorize partial as well as total revocation of a will by physical act. Extrinsic evidence is generally admissible to show whether the testator intended only a partial revocation. In the absence of a statute expressly allowing partial revocation, several states refuse to recognize partial revocation by a physical act. In these jurisdictions, where the testator attempts to revoke a portion of the will, the act is given no effect. Thus, if the testator crosses out a bequest to Tom, Tom takes the bequest despite the attempted cancellation. If the destroyed portion cannot be recreated by extrinsic evidence, only the destroyed portion fails; the remainder of the will is given effect.

4. **Dependent Relative Revocation and Revival.** The doctrine of dependent relative revocation is an equitable doctrine under which a court may disregard a revocation if the court finds that the act of revocation was premised on a mistake of law or fact and would not have occurred but for the testator's mistaken belief that another disposition of property was valid. The requirements of this doctrine are as follows:

(i)   It must be shown that the testator at the time of revocation intended to make a new testamentary disposition that for some reason was ineffective;

(ii) It must be shown that there was an otherwise valid revocation;

(iii) It must be shown that the testator's intent was premised on a mistaken belief as to the validity of the new disposition; and

(iv) It must be shown that invalidation of the revocation would be consistent with the testator's probable intent.

   a.   **Classic pattern--**

LaCroix v. Senecal, 99 A.2d 115 (Conn. 1953).

Facts. Dupre (T) executed a will leaving the residue of her estate in equal shares to her nephew and to her friend, Senecal (D). Approximately two weeks later, T executed a codicil revoking the residuary clause, and replaced it with an almost identical clause with the exception that in the codicil she referred to her nephew by both his nickname (which she had used in the will) and his given name. Senecal's husband witnessed the codicil with two other witnesses. Under statute, the codicil would be valid, but the gift to Senecal would be struck down because her husband was a subscribing witness. T's niece (P), who was left nothing under the will, brought an action for a declaratory judgment to determine whether this gift to D was void. The trial court determined that the bequest to D was valid. P appeals.

Issue. May the doctrine of dependent relative revocation be invoked to sustain a gift by will when the gift became void because of the interest of a subscribing witness to a codicil that substantially confirmed the gift?

Held. Yes. Judgment affirmed.

♦   The doctrine can only be applied where the clear intent of the testator is shown to be that the revocation of the old is made conditional upon the validity of the new. In other words, where the intention to revoke is conditional, but the condition is not fulfilled, the revocation is not effective.

♦   The facts provide no room for doubt that T executed the codicil only to make a name change to remove any uncertainty as to the identification of her nephew.

♦   When we consider the will and the codicil together, which we must do to determine T's intent, it is clear that her intent to revoke the will was conditioned on a codicil that would maintain the same disposition as stated in her residuary clause. Therefore, when D's gift under the codicil became void, T's conditional intent to revoke the will was made inoperative; thus the gift to D in the will continued in effect.

---

b. Doctrine applicable where later will revoked under mistaken belief that doing so reinstates prior will--

---

Estate of Alburn, 118 N.W.2d 919 (Wis. 1963).

Facts. The decedent, Ottilie L. Alburn (T), executed a will in Milwaukee, Wisconsin, in 1955 and left it with her attorney, George R. Affeldt. Thereafter, T moved to Kankakee, Illinois, and in 1959 executed another will while residing there. She then moved to Fort Atkinson, Wisconsin, where she instructed her brother, Edwin Lehmann, to dispose of the Kankakee will, which she had torn up. He did so. Olga Lehmann, the wife of Edwin, testified that T told her that she wanted the Milwaukee will to stand. T's sister, Adele Ruedisili, brought a petition for appointment of a special administrator, alleging that the deceased died intestate. Thereafter, T's grandniece, Viola Henkey, filed a petition for the probate of the Milwaukee will, and Lulu Alburn and Doris Alburn filed a petition for probate of the Kankakee will. The county court heard all three petitions and held that T destroyed the Kankakee will under the mistaken belief that by so doing she would revive the Milwaukee will. The court applied the doctrine of dependent relative revocation and held that the Kankakee will was admitted to probate. Ruedisili appeals.

Issue. When a testator revokes a later will under the mistaken belief that by doing so she is reinstating a prior will, may the doctrine of dependent relative revocation be invoked to render the revocation ineffective?

Held. Yes. Judgment affirmed.

♦ We are committed to the doctrine of dependent relative revocation. The usual situation for application of this doctrine arises when a testator executes one will and thereafter attempts to revoke it by making a later testamentary disposition that for some reason proves ineffective.

♦ However, the doctrine has been applied to the unusual situation in which a testator revokes a later will under the mistaken belief that by doing so she is reinstating a prior will. In this situation, the doctrine of dependent relative revocation is invoked to render the revocation ineffective. The doctrine is based upon the testator's inferred intention. It is held that the destruction of the later document is intended to be conditional when it is accompanied by the express intent of reinstating a former will and there is no explanatory evidence.

♦ Here, we find that the trial court was correct in finding that T had revoked the Kankakee will under the mistaken belief that she was thereby reinstating the prior

Milwaukee will. T's statement to Olga Lehmann that she wished her Milwaukee will to stand, the inference that she did not wish to die intestate, and the fact that she took no steps following the destruction of the Kankakee will to make a new will are sufficient evidence that she destroyed the Kankakee will under the mistaken belief that the Milwaukee will would control the disposition of her estate. Applying the doctrine of dependent relative revocation, therefore, the trial court was correct in holding that the attempted revocation of the Kankakee will was ineffective and admitting the will to probate.

Comment. Wisconsin law on revival of wills precluded the Milwaukee will from being revived.

---

c. **Revival.**

1) **Common law.** The common law rule, still adhered to in several states, is that no part of a will is effective until the death of the testator. Therefore, if Will #2 (which expressly revokes Will #1) is itself revoked before the testator's death, Will #1 alone remains in effect and is operative upon the testator's death. Destruction of Will #2 operates to "revive" Will #1.

2) **Modern law.** In most jurisdictions, a will, once revoked, is not revived unless republished by (i) reexecution or (ii) a later codicil under the doctrine of republication by codicil. Thus, revocation of a later will that contained language revoking an earlier will does not, by itself, revive the earlier will or any of its provisions. Under the UPC and in a substantial minority of states, destruction of Will #2 and its language of revocation may operate to revive Will #1, depending on the testator's intent. Such intent is established by the testator's statements and by reference to all of the circumstances of the case.

5. **Revocation by Operation of Law: Change in Family Circumstances.** A change in family circumstances may revoke a will by operation of law. The law in these instances presumes an intent to revoke on the part of the testator.

a. **Marriage.** At common law, a marriage following the execution of a will had no effect on the will, but a marriage followed by a birth was held to revoke the will. Most states no longer follow the common law rule.

1) **States without statutes.** About half of the states have no statute dealing with the effect of marriage on a previously executed will. In most of these states marriage, by itself, does not affect the will. In a minority of states, however, the courts apply the common law rule noted above.

2) **States with statutes.** In most of the states having statutes dealing with the effect of marriage on a will, the will is only partially revoked. The marriage revokes the will only to the extent of providing the new spouse with an intestate share. After distribution of the spouse's intestate share, the will operates to distribute the remaining assets. In a minority of states, marriage after the execution of a will revokes the will in its entirety. Note that in either case, the will is not partially or totally revoked if (i) the will makes provision for the new spouse, (ii) the will provides that the spouse's omission was intentional, or (iii) it appears that the will was made in contemplation of marriage.

b. **Divorce.** A majority of states have enacted statutes that hold a divorce partially revokes a will in that it automatically revokes the provisions of a will in favor of the former spouse. The will is read as though the former spouse predeceased the testator.

C. COMPONENTS OF A WILL

1. **Integration of Wills.** Integration of a will concerns the problem of what pages should constitute the will. The papers that are present when the will is signed and are intended to be included in the will are integrated. Typically, the problem arises where the pages of a will have not been fastened together.

2. **Republication by Codicil.** Republication by codicil means an implied restatement or rewriting of the language of a valid will as of the time of republication. Republication by codicil has sometimes been used to validate a prior invalid will.

3. **Incorporation by Reference.** Pages that cannot be integrated because they were not present at the will's execution nevertheless may be given effect under the doctrine of incorporation by reference. This doctrine recognizes that a duly executed will may by appropriate reference incorporate into itself any extrinsic document or writing even though the other document was not properly executed. The following requirements must be met:

(i) The document must have been in existence at the time the will was executed;

(ii) The will must expressly refer to the document in the present tense;

(iii) The will must describe the document to be incorporated so clearly that there can be no mistake as to the identity of the document referred to; and

(iv) The testator must have intended to incorporate the extrinsic document as part of the overall testamentary plan.

a. Notebook incorporated by reference--

Clark v. Greenhalge, 582 N.E.2d 949 (Mass. 1991).

Facts. Testatrix, Helen Nesmith (T), executed a will in 1977 naming Greenhalge (D) executor and principal beneficiary of any personal property except that designated by a memorandum known to D or in accord with T's wishes as expressed during T's life. D had helped T draft a document entitled "Memorandum" in 1972; T modified this list of specific bequests from time to time. T wished her friend Clark (P) to have a painting and so listed it in a notebook T kept. T's nurses knew of her wish for P to have the painting and knew of the notebook and had observed T write in it. T executed two codicils in 1980; T amended some bequests and ratified her will in all other respects. Upon T's death, D was given T's notebook. D distributed T's property in accord with the will as amended, the 1972 memorandum, and certain of the provisions in the notebook, including all of the property bequeathed to him in the notebook. However, he refused to give P the painting. P commenced an action to compel D to deliver the painting. The probate court found: (i) T wished P to have the painting; (ii) the notebook was a memorandum within the meaning of T's will; (iii) the notebook was in existence at the time of the codicils, which ratified the language of the will in its entirety; and (iv) the notebook was incorporated by reference into the terms of the will. D appeals.

Issue. Was T's notebook incorporated by reference into the terms of T's will?

Held. Yes. Judgment affirmed.

♦ A will may incorporate by reference any document not so executed and witnessed if it was in existence when the will was executed and is identified by clear and satisfactory proof as the paper referred to in the will.

♦ The cardinal rule in the interpretation of wills is that the intention of the testator shall prevail. T's language and the circumstances surrounding the execution of T's will and codicils are used to determine T's intent.

♦ T intended to retain the right to alter and amend her bequests of tangible personal property in her will without having to formally amend the will. The mechanism T chose was a memorandum, and the notebook, although not titled "Memorandum," has as its purpose and is in the spirit of T's intent. T is not limited to only one memorandum.

♦ Having been in existence at the time T executed her codicils, that republishing of T's intent incorporated the notebook by reference.

---

b. Validation of inoperative will by holographic codicil--

Facts. The will of the decedent, Dexter G. Johnson (T), consisted of a single sheet of paper with three typewritten paragraphs. The typewritten portion was not dated, signed, or attested by two witnesses. At the bottom of the typewritten portion, T wrote in his handwriting a $10 bequest to his brother James. The proponents of the will introduced evidence showing that T was a practicing attorney who had prepared many wills; that he had told his insurance counselor that he had a will but it was out of date; that he had told his rental agent that the typewritten instrument was his will and that he wanted his rental agent to witness it; that his rental agent did not do so but later T told him that he had changed his will by codicil and did not need him to sign it as a witness. The trial court refused to admit the instrument to probate. The appellate court affirmed. The proponents appeal.

Issue. May a valid holographic codicil republish and validate a will that was theretofore inoperative because it was not signed, dated, or attested according to law?

Held. Yes. Judgment reversed and the case remanded with directions to enter the will for probate.

◆   There is no question that the typewritten instrument was not signed, dated, or attested. A will may be so defective, as here, that it is not entitled to probate, but if testamentary in character it is a will nonetheless.

◆   By definition a codicil is a supplement to an existing will made by the testator to alter, enlarge, or restrict its provisions and it must be testamentary in character. A codicil need not be called a codicil; rather, it is the intention to add a codicil that is controlling. Here, the handwritten words are testamentary in character and they make an addition to the provisions of the will already in existence. Further, the codicil meets all of the requirements of a valid holographic codicil. It is written, dated, and signed by T. The fact that it was written on the same piece of paper as the typewritten will does not invalidate the codicil.

◆   The general rule is that a codicil validly executed operates as a republication of the will no matter what defects may have existed in the execution of the earlier document, that the instruments are incorporated as one, and that a proper execution of the codicil extends also to the will. We therefore hold that the valid holographic codicil incorporated the prior will by reference and republished and validated the prior will as of the date of the codicil.

Concurrence. All rules of construction are designed for the purpose of effectuating the intent of the testator. To hold otherwise would permit a contrary disposition of the testator's property against the purpose for which the statutory provisions were aimed.

Dissent. The typewritten part is not a will and the handwritten part is not a codicil. T intended the typewritten portion to be part of his will, not the completed will. I can never subscribe to the proposition that a holographic codicil will validate as a will an instrument that is typewritten, unfinished, undated, unsigned, and unattested. Property may descend by will when the will is executed in conformity with the statutes.

---

4. **Acts of Independent Significance.** Under the UPC, a will may dispose of property by reference to acts and events that have significance apart from their effect on the dispositions made in the will (*e.g.,* "I devise Blackacre to the persons named as beneficiaries in my sister's will.")

D. CONTRACTS RELATING TO WILLS

Contracts to make a will, contracts not to revoke a will, and contracts not to make a will are kinds of contracts pertaining to wills. In these instances, the law of contracts applies. A will in violation of a valid contract made by the testator, while it may be probated, will be subject to contractual remedies (*e.g.,* imposition of constructive trust).

1. **Contracts to Make a Will.** Many states have enacted statutes requiring that a contract to make a gift by will be in writing. If the promisor fails to make the promised testamentary gift, the promisee has a cause of action against the promisor's estate for damages for breach of contract. The measure of damages is the value of the property promised to be devised or bequeathed. However, if the case involves a promise to make a devise or bequest of specific property, the usual remedy is to grant a constructive trust for the promisee's benefit.

2. **Contracts Not to Revoke a Will.** These contracts typically arise when a husband and wife have executed joint or mutual wills. A number of states have enacted statutes requiring that any agreement relating to a will, including a contract not to revoke a will, be in a writing executed with certain formalities. The mere execution of reciprocal wills containing identical provisions does not constitute evidence that the wills were contractual.

3. **Joint Wills.** A joint will is the will of two or more persons executed as a single testamentary instrument. In contrast to joint wills, reciprocal wills, sometimes called mirror wills, are separate wills of two or more persons containing reciprocal provisions.

    a. **Elective share in conflict with will contract--**

Via v. Putnam, 626 So. 2d 460 (Fla. 1995).

Facts. Edgar and Joann Putnam executed mutual wills contracting that the survivor not do anything to defeat the distribution schedule set forth therein. The wills devised the spouse's entire estate to the survivor and the residuary estate to the children upon the survivor's death. After Joann died, Edgar remarried and did not execute a subsequent will providing for his new wife, Rachel Putnam (P). Upon Edgar's death, P filed a petition to determine the share of a pretermitted spouse and an election to take her elective share. The children of the first marriage (Ds) filed claims against the estate alleging that by marrying again, Edgar had violated his contract not to defeat the distribution schedule set forth in his mutual will. The trial judge found that the mutual will constituted a binding contract and Ds were third-party beneficiaries to that contract. Summary judgment was entered for Ds, who were found to be class 7 obligations under Florida Law (third-party beneficiaries/creditor status), and the judge concluded that P's pretermitted or elective share is subject to the class 7 obligations of the estate. The second district court of appeal reversed, acknowledging that its decision conflicts with the third district's ruling in *Johnson v. Girtman*, 542 So. 2d 1033 (Fla. 3d DCA 1989). Ds appeal.

Issue. Should the claims of the decedent's children as third-party beneficiaries under the mutual wills of their parents be given creditor status under Florida law when their interests contravene the interests of the surviving spouse under the pretermitted spouse statute?

Held. No. Judgment affirmed.

- We agree with the district court's reliance on the reasoning in *Shrimp v. Huff*, 315 Md. 624, 556 A.2d 252 (1989), a case identical to this one. The *Shrimp* court found the public policy underlying the marriage relationship and the elective share statute required it to rule in favor of protecting the surviving spouse's right to receive an elective share. The district court found that Florida's statutes also suggest the same strong public policy. The third district in *Johnson* took the view that the surviving spouse's statutory share can be subordinated to claims of third-party beneficiaries of previously executed mutual wills. *Johnson* and other similar rulings have advanced four rationales for giving priority to contract beneficiaries: (i) the surviving spouse's rights attach only to property legally and equitably owned by the deceased spouse, and the will contract places equitable title in the contract beneficiary; (ii) when the surviving testator accepts benefits under the contractual will, an equitable trust on the property is created in favor of the contract beneficiaries; the testator is entitled only to a life estate and the beneficiaries take the remainder upon the testator's death; (iii) when the surviving testator benefits under the contractual will, the testator becomes estopped from making a different disposition of the property, despite a later marriage; and (iv) when the surviving testator breaches the will contract, the beneficiaries are entitled to judgment creditor status. Under these theories, the duration of the marriage makes no difference.

- We, like the court in *Shrimp*, recognize the well-established principle that contracts that discourage or restrain the right to marry are void as against public policy.

- The Florida legislature set forth three specific circumstances when a pretermitted spouse would not be entitled to a share of the decedent's estate: (i) when the spouse has been provided for or waived provision by prenuptial or postnuptial agreement; (ii) when the spouse is provided for in the will; and (iii) when the will states an intention not to provide for the spouse. The trial court found none of these exceptions applied. For us to hold otherwise would amend the statutory exceptions and add a fourth. We have no authority to do so.

———————————

V. NONPROBATE TRANSFERS AND PLANNING FOR INCAPACITY

A. REVOCABLE TRUSTS

1. **Introduction.** In a revocable trust the settlor has the power to revoke, alter, or amend the trust and has the right to trust income during her lifetime. Revocable trusts are valid in all jurisdictions.

2. **Retention of Control by Settlor.** If the settlor retains numerous powers and lacks the true trust "intent," the trust may be ruled illusory. However, as long as the trust creates some interests in some category of beneficiaries, courts will recognize a valid nontestamentary trust even though the settlor retains extensive powers.

    a. **Creation of valid inter vivos trust notwithstanding control retained by settlor/trustee--**

Farkas v. Williams, 125 N.E.2d 600 (Ill. 1955).

Facts. Albert B. Farkas, who died intestate, purchased on four occasions during his life the stock of Investors Mutual, Inc., instructing it, by means of a written application, to issue the stock in his name "as trustee for Richard J. Williams." Farkas also signed separate declarations of trust, all of which were identical except as to dates. In each of these declarations, Farkas reserved to himself as settlor the following powers: (i) the right to receive during his lifetime all cash dividends; (ii) the right at any time to change the beneficiary or revoke the trust; and (iii) upon sale or redemption of any portion of the trust property, the right to retain the proceeds therefrom for his own use. The co-administrators of the estate (Ps) bring this action to have declared their legal rights in the four stock certificates. The circuit court found that the declarations were testamentary in character and, not having been executed with the formalities of a will, were invalid, and directed that the stock be awarded to Ps as assets of the estate of Albert Farkas. The appellate court affirmed. Williams and Investors Mutual (Ds) appeal.

Issues.

(i) Does the fact that the interest of a beneficiary is contingent upon a certain state of facts existing at the time of the settlor's death indicate that no present interest is acquired in the subject matter of a trust, and hence render a trust instrument testamentary in character?

(ii) Does the retention of power by a settlor to sell or redeem stock and keep the proceeds for his own use, to change the beneficiary, and to revoke the trust indicate that the settlor has retained such control over the subject matter of a trust so as to render a trust instrument testamentary in character?

Held. (i) No. (ii) No. Judgment reversed and case remanded.

♦ Williams acquired a present interest in the subject matter of the intended trusts. Farkas, immediately after execution of these instruments, could not deal with the stock the same as if he owned the property absolutely. As trustee, Farkas is held to have intended to take on those obligations that are expressly set out in the instrument, as well as those fiduciary obligations implied by law.

> The fact that the trust instrument provides that "the decease of the beneficiary before my death shall operate as a revocation of this trust" does not change the result. The disposition is not testamentary and the intended trust is valid even though the interest of the beneficiary is contingent upon the existence of a certain state of facts at the time of the settlor's death.

> Admittedly, absent this provision, Williams's interest would have been greater. But to say that his interest would have been greater is not to say that he did not have a beneficial interest during the lifetime of Farkas.

♦ Farkas did not retain such control over the subject matter of the trust as to render the trust instruments testamentary in character. The retention by the settlor of the power to revoke, even when coupled with a reservation of a life interest in the trust property, does not render the trust inoperative for want of execution of a will.

> A more difficult problem is posed by the fact that Farkas is also trustee and as such is empowered to vote, sell, and otherwise deal in and with the subject matter of the trusts. Here, the control reserved is not as great as in those cases where the power is reserved to the owner as settlor, for as trustee he must conduct himself in accordance with standards applicable to trustees generally. Williams would have had an enforceable claim against Farkas's estate were Farkas to have improperly dissipated the stock.

> Another factor in determining whether an inter vivos trust exists is the formality of the transaction. Here, the stock certificates in question were issued in Farkas's name as trustee for Williams. He thus manifested his intention in a solemn and formal manner.

---

b. **Inter vivos trust not revoked under presumption applicable to wills.** *In re Estate and Trust of Pilafas*, 836 P.2d 420 (Ariz. 1992), involved the common law presumption that if a will is last seen in a testator's possession and cannot be found after his death, the testator destroyed the will.

The decedent in this case, Pilafas, executed a will and a revocable inter vivos trust, appointing himself as trustee. He updated the will and the trust twice, and his lawyer gave him the final will and the revised trust before Pilafas's death. However, after he died, his son unsuccessfully searched his house for the documents. Because of the presumption, the court held that Pilafas revoked his will. On the other hand, a trust, unlike a will, involves the present transfer of a property interest to beneficiaries. These interests can only be taken from the beneficiaries in accordance with a trust provision, by the beneficiaries' own acts, or by a court decree. Pilafas's trust provided for revocation only by written instrument. Therefore, the court held that the inter vivos trust was not revoked.

   c. **Creditors may reach trust assets over which the settlor had control at the time of his death.** In *State Street Bank & Trust Co. v. Reiser*, 389 N.E.2d 768 (Mass. 1979), the decedent, Wilfred Dunnebier, had created an inter vivos trust with the power to amend or revoke the trust, and conveyed to the trust the capital stock of five closely held corporations. The following year, Dunnebier borrowed $75,000 from the State Street Bank in the form of an unsecured loan. He died four months later, and his estate had insufficient assets to pay the entire indebtedness due the bank. The bank then sought to reach the assets of the inter vivos trust. Because Dunnebier's trust was self-settled and its entire corpus was available to him, the bank could have reached the entire trust corpus to satisfy Dunnebier's debt before his death. Finding that creditors should also be able to reach property placed in such a trust after death, the court held that where a person places property in trust and reserves the right to amend and revoke, or to direct disposition of principal and income, the settlor's creditors may reach, in satisfaction of the settlor's debts to them, those assets owned by the trust over which the settlor had such control at the time of his death as would have enabled the settlor to use the trust assets for his own benefit.

      1) **UPC position.** If probate assets are insufficient, UPC section 6-215 allows creditors to reach a decedent's payable-on-death accounts and his joint bank accounts.

3. **Testamentary "Pour-Over" into an Inter Vivos Trust.** Pour-over wills are useful to establish an inter vivos trust, which later merges into the estate after the death of the settlor. The settlor creates a revocable inter vivos trust by naming a trustee and then transferring probate assets to that trustee. The settlor then executes a will devising the residue of his estate to the trustee, to hold as trustee under the terms of the trust.

   a. **Uniform Testamentary Additions to Trusts Act.** This Act validates a testamentary gift to a trust provided the trust is sufficiently described in the testator's will. The trust instrument may be executed after the will.

This is so whether the trust was created by the testator or by a third person and whether it was modifiable or in fact modified. The size and extent of the trust corpus during the testator's lifetime is likewise immaterial. The Act specifically validates gifts to either funded or unfunded life insurance trusts, even if the testator has reserved all rights of ownership in the policies.

b. **Effect of divorce on validity of dispositions to former spouse made by revocable inter vivos trust.** *Clymer v. Mayo*, 473 N.E.2d 1084 (Mass. 1985), concerned the testator's implied intent. In 1973, Clara Mayo executed a will and a revocable trust. Under the will, the bulk of her estate was to pour over into the revocable trust, of which James Mayo, Clara's husband, was the principal beneficiary. The Mayos divorced in 1978, and the question raised after Clara's death in 1981 was whether the Massachusetts statute that revokes any disposition to a former spouse made by a will applies to revoke dispositions to the former spouse made by a revocable inter vivos trust that has no funding or practical significance until the decedent's death. The court concluded that in the absence of an expressed contrary intent, the statute applies to these circumstances.

4. **Use of Revocable Trusts in Estate Planning.**

a. **Consequences during life of settlor.** During the life of the settlor, a revocable trust may be used to relieve the settlor of the burdens of financial management, to deal with the contingency of the settlor's incompetency, and to clarify title and ownership of assets. There are no federal tax advantages in creating a revocable trust, since trust income is taxable to the settlor regardless of to whom it is paid.

b. **Consequences at death of settlor.** Upon the death of the settlor, a revocable trust can be used to avoid probate. Under a revocable trust continuing after the settlor's death, income and principal can be disbursed to the beneficiaries without significant delay. In contrast to probate, there is no short-term statute of limitations applicable to revocable trusts to cut off the rights of creditors. A revocable trust avoids publicity since it is not recorded in a public place. To avoid ancillary probate over real property located outside the domiciliary state, land in another state can be transferred to a revocable inter vivos trust. In some states, the law might permit a funded revocable trust to defeat a spouse's elective share in certain circumstances. An inter vivos trust of personal property may be governed by the state law of the settlor's choice. In practice, it is more difficult to set aside a revocable trust than a will on grounds of lack of mental capacity and undue influence. Finally, a revocable trust that becomes irrevocable upon the death of one spouse can thereby control the surviving spouse's disposition of property.

B. CONTRACTS WITH PAYABLE-ON-DEATH PROVISIONS

1. **Life Insurance.** The issue in these cases includes whether a beneficiary of a life insurance policy can be changed by will. A majority of courts hold that if the policy requires written notice of change of beneficiary filed with the insurance company, the beneficiary of a life insurance policy may not be changed by will.

2. **Nontestamentary Transfers at Death.** Under the UPC, written agreements to pay, after the death of the decedent, money or other benefits to a person designated by the decedent in either the instrument or a separate writing are deemed to be nontestamentary.

3. **Successor Beneficiary Not Permitted in Life Insurance Contract--**

Wilhoit v. Peoples Life Insurance Co., 218 F.2d 887 (7th Cir. 1955).

Facts. Roley Wilhoit was the insured of a $5,000 life insurance policy issued by Century Life and reinsured by Peoples Life (D1). After Roley's death in 1930, Sarah Wilhoit, his widow and beneficiary, arranged to leave the amount due her on deposit with D1 on specified terms, including that upon her death any remaining funds plus accrued interest would be paid to her brother, Robert Owens. Robert Owens died in 1932, leaving all of his property by will to Thomas Owens (D2). Sarah Wilhoit died in 1951. Her will purported to leave the funds on deposit with D1 to Robert Wilhoit (P). Both P and D2 claim the funds; D1 refused to recognize P's claim. The district court granted P's motion for summary judgment, and D2 appeals.

Issue. Where the proceeds of a life insurance policy are to be disposed of in accordance with its provisions, may a beneficiary of the policy designate a successor beneficiary to take upon the death of the primary beneficiary?

Held. No. Judgment affirmed.

♦ Ds rely on cases that have held that the proceeds of a life insurance policy are to be disposed of in accordance with its provisions, and that a beneficiary, if authorized by the policy, may designate a successor beneficiary to take on the death of the primary beneficiary. This contention is without merit if we do not accept the premise that the agreement between Sarah Wilhoit and the company was an insurance contract or an agreement thereto. We reject this premise and hold that the arrangement between the parties was the result of a separate and independent agreement, unrelated to the terms of the policy.

♦ Sarah Wilhoit did not take advantage of the investment provision in the insurance policy by which she could have left the proceeds with the company on the terms and conditions stated therein. Instead, she accepted the proceeds and surrendered the policy. Only later did she by letter make her own proposal, which was accepted by the company on conditions that differed materially from those contained in the policy. We agree with P, therefore, that the provision in the agreement by which Robert Owens was to take the funds in the event of her death was an invalid testamentary disposition.

♦ Finally, it is not immaterial to take into consideration the intentions of the parties. Here, Sarah Wilhoit in her will specifically devised the funds in controversy to P. It thus appears plain that she did not intend the funds to go to the successors of Robert Owens but that, after his death, she thought she had a right to dispose of the funds as she saw fit. While we recognize that the intention of the parties is not controlling, we think that it is entitled to some consideration.

---

4. Investment Club Proceeds--

Estate of Hillowitz, 238 N.E.2d 723 (N.Y. 1968).

Facts. Abraham Hillowitz's (T's) executors (Ps) brought a discovery proceeding in surrogate court against T's widow (D) to have determined whether T's investment club contract to have his share paid to his widow upon his death was an invalid attempt to make a testamentary disposition of property. The surrogate court ruled for D; the appellate division ruled for Ps. D appeals.

Issue. Is a partnership agreement providing that, upon the death of one partner, his interest will pass to the surviving partner or partners, resting in contract, valid?

Held. Yes. Order reversed.

♦ There is no difference between a contract providing for surviving partner(s) and one providing for a surviving widow.

♦ This is a third-party beneficiary contract, performable at death, and it need not conform to the requirements of the statute of wills.

♦ Other such contracts include (i) a contract to make a will, (ii) an inter vivos trust in which the settlor reserves a life estate, and (iii) an insurance policy.

---

5. **Change of Beneficiary of Life Insurance Policy by Will.** In *Cook v. Equitable Life Assurance Society*, 428 N.E.2d 110 (Ind. App. 1981), the life insurance policy of the decedent, Cook, named his ex-wife as beneficiary. Although Cook remarried and had a son with his new wife, he never provided written notice to change the beneficiary as required by the insurance company. However, he did

leave a holographic will leaving his life insurance policy to his wife and son. Thus, the issue was whether the beneficiary of a life insurance policy could be changed by the testator's intent as expressed in his will. The court held that an insured's attempt to change the beneficiary of a life insurance policy by will, without more, is ineffectual. The court stated that it is in the interest of insurance companies to require and to follow specified procedures in the change of beneficiaries so that they may pay benefits to persons properly entitled to them without subjecting themselves to claims by others of whose rights they had no notice or knowledge. These procedures are also in the interest of beneficiaries themselves, since insurance companies will not feel obligated to withhold payment until a will has been probated, in fear of litigation that might result from having paid the wrong party.

6. ERISA Plans--

Egelhoff v. Egelhoff, 532 U.S. 141 (2001).

Facts. When the Egelhoffs divorced, David was employed by Boeing and had designated Donna (D) as the beneficiary under his pension plan and his life insurance policy, both governed by the Employee Retirement Income Security Act of 1974 ("ERISA"). Two months after the divorce, David died intestate. The life insurance proceeds were paid to D. David's children by a previous marriage (Ps) sued D to recover the insurance proceeds, relying on a state statute that provides that, upon divorce, a provision for the payment at death of the decedent's interest in nonprobate assets to a former spouse is revoked. In a separate action, Ps also sued to recover the pension plan benefits. The state supreme court found for Ps. The Supreme Court granted certiorari.

Issue. Does ERISA preempt a state statute that provides that the designation of a spouse as the beneficiary of a nonprobate asset is revoked automatically upon divorce to the extent that it applies to ERISA plans?

Held. Yes. Judgment reversed and case remanded.

◆　ERISA's preemption provision states that ERISA "shall supersede any and all State laws insofar as they may now or hereafter relate to any employee benefit plan" covered by ERISA.

◆　A state law relates to an ERISA plan if "it has a connection with or reference to such a plan." To determine whether there is "a connection," we look to both the objectives of the ERISA statute, as a guide in identifying the scope of the state law that Congress understood would survive, and to the nature of the effect of the state law on ERISA plans.

◆　Here, the state statute mandates that ERISA plan administrators follow particular rules for determining beneficiary status; *i.e.*, pay beneficiaries indicated by state law rather than those in the plan documents. This provision is contrary to ERISA's demands that a plan must "specify the basis on which payments are made to and from the plan" and that the administrator must look to the documents and instruments governing the plan when administering it.

♦ The state plan also interferes with nationally uniform administration of ERISA plans.

♦ While the state statute protects administrators from liability for making payments to the named beneficiary unless they have "actual knowledge" of the dissolution of the marriage, and it permits them to refuse to make payments until any dispute among possible beneficiaries is resolved, this transfers the costs of delay to the beneficiaries and requires administrators to be familiar with the laws of all of the states.

Dissent (Breyer, J.). We have previously found that the fact that state law "imposes some burden on the administration of ERISA plans" does not necessarily require preemption. State laws such as the one at issue here provide for what the worker likely would have wanted. While the worker could have changed the beneficiary, many are not aware of the provision, do not understand it, and have no time to change the beneficiary. The divorced wife acquired her fair share during the divorce proceeding.

C. JOINT TENANCY AND MULTIPLE-PARTY BANK ACCOUNTS

1. **Types of Accounts.** Multiple-party bank accounts include joint and survivor accounts, payable-on-death accounts, agency accounts, and savings account trusts.

2. **Joint Bank Account: Lack of Donative Intent.** In *Franklin v. Anna National Bank of Anna*, 488 N.E.2d 1117 (Ill. 1986), the executor of the decedent's estate brought an action to acquire the funds of a joint account that had been in the name of Frank Whitehead, the decedent, and Cora Goddard, the sister of Whitehead's deceased wife. Goddard had moved in with Whitehead to help him because his eyesight was failing. Although Goddard alleged that Whitehead wanted her to have the money in the account if she outlived him, she testified that she did not deposit money in the account and made no withdrawals. Furthermore, when the executor replaced Goddard as Whitehead's primary caretaker, Whitehead wrote a letter to the bank, attempting to have the executor's name added to the savings account and Goddard's name removed. However, the bank would not remove a signature from the signature card based on a letter, so the most recent signature card the bank had for the account was signed by Whitehead and Goddard. On appeal, the court stated that the form of a joint tenancy agreement is not conclusive regarding the intention of the depositors between themselves, but the one claiming adversely has the burden of establishing by clear and convincing evidence that a gift was not intended. Here, the

evidence established that Whitehead had made Goddard a signatory of the joint account for his own convenience, in case he could not get his money, and not with the intent to effect a gift. Thus, the court held that the joint tenancy was severed and that the money in the joint account was the property of Whitehead's estate.

D. JOINT TENANCIES IN REALTY

One common method of avoiding the cost and delay of probate is to hold property in joint tenancy or tenancy by the entirety. When one joint tenant or tenant by the entirety dies, the survivor owns the property outright. The share of a joint tenant cannot be devised by will. If a joint tenant does not want the co-tenant to take his share at death, he must sever the joint tenancy during his lifetime, thus creating a tenancy in common. Creditors of a joint tenant can reach the joint tenant's interest only during his life.

E. PLANNING FOR INCAPACITY

1. **The Durable Power of Attorney.** A durable power of attorney may be used to plan for incapacity.

   a. **Agent's action upheld.** *Franzen v. Norwest Bank Colorado*, 955 P.2d 1018 (Colo. 1998), involved an agent's authority to revoke a trust. Mrs. Franzen, a nursing home resident and the beneficiary of a trust, gave her brother, O'Brien, a power of attorney that included the power to revoke trusts. When O'Brien attempted to revoke the trust, the bank that had been named trustee filed a petition for advice and a petition for appointment of a conservator to protect Mrs. Franzen's assets. The probate court found that the power of attorney had created a valid agency but that the trust continued in existence. The bank was appointed special fiduciary with responsibility for both trust and non-trust assets. The court of appeals reversed, and the bank appealed. The Colorado Supreme Court affirmed, stating that although under Colorado's power of attorney statute an agent may not revoke a trust without specific reference to the trust in the power of attorney, that statute went into effect almost two years after Mrs. Franzen executed the power of attorney, and there is no common law rule that requires a power of attorney to refer to a trust by name. Thus, the court concluded that although the language in the power of attorney executed by Mrs. Franzen did not specifically mention the trust by name, it expressly authorized O'Brien to revoke the trust.

      1) **Potential for abuse.** The *Franzen* holding gives the attorney-in-fact the power to change the will once the principal becomes incompetent. An attorney who drafts such a broad power may unleash a dangerous weapon in the hands of an unscrupulous individual.

2. **Directives Regarding Health Care and Disposition of the Body.**

   a. **Advance directives: living wills, health care proxies, and hybrids.** In *Cruzan v. Director, Missouri Department of Health*, 497 U.S. 261 (1990), the Supreme Court held that a person may make known her desires regarding termination of medical treatment, or may appoint an agent to make those decisions, providing state law requirements are met.

   1) **Three types of advance directives.** To resolve conflicts over the wishes of an incompetent person, the law relies on advance directives and, in the absence of directives, default rules. There are three basic types of advance directives.

      a) **Livings wills.** A living will specifies how an individual wants to be treated in end-of-life situations or in the event of incompetence.

      b) **Health care proxies.** A health care proxy, or durable power of attorney for health care, designates an agent to make health care decisions for the patient.

      c) **Hybrids.** A hybrid incorporates both of the first two approaches, allowing the individual to direct treatment preferences and designate an agent to make substituted decisions.

   2) **Absence of advance directives.** In an end-of-life situation where there is no advance directive, responsibility for an incompetent patient's health care decisions usually goes to the patient's spouse or next of kin, subject to the state's interest in preserving life.

      a) **State law unconstitutional--**

Bush v. Schiavo, 885 So. 2d 321 (Fla. 2004).

Facts. In 1990, after suffering a cardiac arrest and being rushed to the hospital, 27-year-old Theresa Schiavo failed to regain consciousness. She lived in nursing homes, needed constant care, and was fed and hydrated by tubes. In 1998, Theresa's husband, Michael, petitioned the guardianship court to authorize the termination of life-prolonging procedures. Theresa's parents opposed the petition. After a trial, the court issued an order authorizing the discontinuance of artificial life support. The district court affirmed, finding that the trial court had clear and convincing evidence to support its determination that, after 10 years in a persistent vegetative state, Theresa would elect to stop the life-prolonging procedures if she were competent to choose. Two years of further litigation resulted in the trial court's decision being upheld. Theresa's nutrition and hydration tube was removed in 2003. Six days later, the Florida legislature passed a law allowing the governor to stay the removal of the nutrition tube on facts that matched Theresa's case.

The governor issued an executive order, and Theresa's tube was reinserted. After Michael was successful in lower court challenges to the statute, the Florida Supreme Court issued its decision.

Issue. Is a law constitutional if it authorizes the executive branch to interfere with the final judicial determination in a case?

Held. No. Judgment affirmed.

♦ Separation of powers in our state constitution provides that the judiciary is a co-equal branch of the government with the sole authority to exercise judicial power. Absent a constitutional amendment, the legislature cannot reallocate the balance of power.

♦ The United States Supreme Court has explained that the judiciary is subject to review only by superior courts. The governor has no authority to review the accuracy of judicial decisions.

♦ Here, the issue of discontinuance of life support was fully litigated. The act that permitted the governor to reverse a properly rendered final judgment constituted an unconstitutional encroachment on the power reserved for the judiciary. The act is unconstitutional as applied in this case.

♦ The act is also unconstitutional on its face because it delegates legislative power to the governor. The legislature did not provide any standards by which the governor, in any case, should determine whether a stay should be issued, how long it should remain in effect, or what criteria should be applied for lifting the stay. This absolute discretion to decide whether to issue a stay and when to lift it makes the governor's decision virtually unreviewable. If the judicial branch were subordinated to the final directive of the other branches, no court judgment would be truly final.

---

b. **Disposition of decedent's body.** All states have enacted Uniform Anatomical Gift Acts, which allow a person to donate his body to any hospital, physician, or medical school for research or transplantation.

VI. CONSTRUCTION OF WILLS

A. MISTAKEN OR AMBIGUOUS LANGUAGE IN WILLS

In general, extrinsic evidence is not admissible to change the plain meaning of a will. Some jurisdictions do not apply this rule rigidly but invoke a presumption that can be overcome with strong evidence of a contrary meaning. Parol evidence may be admissible to resolve ambiguities in a will.

1. **Latent Ambiguities.** A latent ambiguity exists when the language of the will, though clear on its face, is susceptible to more than one meaning when applied to the extrinsic facts. In these cases, parol evidence is admissible to resolve the ambiguity.

2. **Patent Ambiguities.** A patent ambiguity exists when the uncertainty appears on the face of the will. The traditional view is that parol evidence is not admissible to clarify a patent ambiguity. The modern trend is to admit parol evidence in these instances as well.

3. **No Extrinsic Evidence to Correct Drafter's Mistake--**

Mahoney v. Grainger, 186 N.E. 86 (Mass. 1933).

Facts. Upon Sullivan's (T's) death, her only heir at law was her aunt. However, shortly before T's death, T executed a will, instructing her attorney to leave the residue of her estate to her 25 cousins and "let them share equally." The language of the residue clause read: "I give, devise and bequeath to my heirs at law living at the time of my decease, absolutely; to be divided among them equally, share and share alike." The probate court denied a petition for distribution to the first cousins. Certain cousins appeal.

Issue. Are T's statements regarding T's understanding of "heirs at law" admissible?

Held. No. Decree affirmed.

♦ A testator's statements are admissible only to give evidence where testamentary language is not clear in its application to the facts. Extrinsic evidence will not be allowed if the property bequeathed or the identity of the beneficiary is clearly and absolutely identified.

♦ There is no doubt as to the meaning of "heirs at law." A drafter's mistake does not authorize a court to reform or alter a duly executed and allowed will.

Comment. This holding was reaffirmed in 1977 in *Gustafson v. Svenson*, 366 N.E.2d 761 (Mass. 1977).

4.   Recourse for Erroneous Description--

Arnheiter v. Arnheiter, 125 A.2d 914 (N.J. 1956)

Facts. Burnette Guterl (T) died leaving a will that provided for the sale of her undivided one-half interest in property located at 304 Harrison Avenue and use of the proceeds for trusts for her nieces. In fact, T did not own any property at that address. She owned an undivided one-half interest in property at 317 Harrison Avenue. Her executrix applies to the superior court to correct the mistake.

Issue. If the description of property in a will consists of several particulars that do not match any one piece of property, may the less essential particulars be rejected if the remainder of the description clearly identifies a particular piece of property?

Held. Yes. Judgment construing will.

♦   A court cannot reform a will by changing any of the language in the will or by substituting or adding words.

♦   The principle of "*falsa demonstratio non nocet*" (mere erroneous description does not vitiate), however, applies to the situation at hand.

♦   T owned only one piece of property on Harrison at the time she drafted the will and at the time of her death, and she made no other provision for the property at 317 Harrison. If we disregard the street number in the will, we are led to the conclusion that even without a number, the remaining description is sufficient to identify the property passing under the will.

5.   **Correcting Mistakes.** If the alleged mistake involves the reasons that led the testator to make the will (or the reasons for making or not making a particular gift), and the mistake was not fraudulently induced, no relief is granted. Some courts have recognized an exception if the mistake appears on the face of the will, and the disposition the testator would have made but for the mistake can at least be inferred from the instrument. Cases in which such relief is granted are rare because it is unlikely for the mistake and the alternate disposition to appear on the face of the instrument. If a provision was mistakenly omitted from the will, or a provision contained in the will is not what the testator intended, parol testimony is generally not admissible to show the existence of the mistake and what the testator intended to provide had the mistake not been made. Thus, mistakes of omission generally cannot be corrected, nor can a mistake in describing a beneficiary or item of property.

a.   **Extrinsic evidence of scrivener's error admissible to ascertain testator's true intent--**

Erickson v. Erickson, 716 A.2d 92 (Conn. 1998).

Facts. The decedent, Ronald Erickson, executed a will two days before he married Dorothy Erickson (D). The will left everything to D. If she predeceased him, half of Ronald's estate was to go to his children and half to D's children. D was appointed guardian of Ronald's children (whose mother had died) and executor of his estate. Ronald's attorney innocently misrepresented that the will would be valid after the marriage to D, but the will did not contain any language providing for the contingency of the subsequent marriage. (Connecticut law provides that if a testator marries subsequent to the making of a will and the will makes no provision for such a contingency, the marriage operates as a revocation of the will.) Eleven years later, upon Ronald's death, the will was admitted for probate. Ronald's daughter, Alicia Erickson (P), appealed. Prior to trial, P filed a motion in limine to exclude extrinsic evidence of Ronald's intent. D made a detailed offer of proof to show Ronald's contrary intent. The trial court granted P's motion, but dismissed P's appeal, and found that the will provided for the contingency of marriage. P appeals. D cross appeals.

Issue. Should the trial court have admitted extrinsic evidence regarding the decedent's intent that his will would not be revoked automatically by his subsequent marriage?

Held. Yes. Judgment reversed and case remanded.

♦   The nature of the will's provisions and the couple's extreme closeness at the time of marriage provide clear and convincing evidence of the provision for the contingency of marriage even though the will itself did not do so and, under existing case law, would have been revoked by a subsequent marriage.

♦   We have previously held that extrinsic evidence is not admissible, but conclude now that the reasoning of the dissent in *Connecticut Junior Republic v. Sharon Hospital*, 188 Conn. 1, 448 A.2d 190 (1982), is persuasive and we overrule that case.

♦   If a scrivener's error has misled the testator into executing a will on the belief that it will be valid notwithstanding the testator's subsequent marriage, extrinsic evidence of that error is admissible to establish the intent of the testator that his will be valid notwithstanding the subsequent marriage.

♦   If the error and the testator's intent are established by clear and convincing evidence, they will be sufficient to establish that the will has provided for such contingency.

♦   Extrinsic evidence is admissible to prove fraud, duress, or undue influence. There is little difference between erroneous beliefs induced by fraud, duress, or undue influence and those induced by innocent error, as here. In both situations, the influence of a third party distorts the process.

♦   There is no subversion of the policy of the statute of wills excluding extrinsic evidence because of the risk of subversion of the testator's intent, where the testator cannot personally defend his testamentary bequest. That statute would not exclude extrinsic evidence where fraud, duress, or undue influence were concerned. Therefore, that statute does not compel enforcement of testamentary provisions that the testator never intended to make.

♦ If fraud were involved, it is arguable that the beneficiaries of the fraudulent conduct would not be allowed to benefit and a constructive trust would be imposed on their inheritance. Analogously, here, extrinsic evidence should be admissible to establish the testator's true intent.

---

6. **Liability for Drafting Ambiguous Will.** If, in preparing a will pursuant to the testator's instructions, the attorney omits a clause that makes a gift to a beneficiary, the attorney is liable to the intended beneficiary for the amount the beneficiary would have received under the will had the clause not been negligently omitted. Case law, however, has held that an attorney is not liable for drafting an *ambiguous* document.

7. **Parol Allowed to Contradict Statements in Will.** In *Fleming v. Morrison*, 72 N.E. 499 (Mass. 1904), Francis Butterfield had executed a sham will leaving all of his property to Fleming in an effort to get her to sleep with him. The will was drafted by Butterfield's attorney, who also attested the will as one of the witnesses. Butterfield informed his attorney that the will was fake and was made for a specific purpose. When the will was admitted to probate, the court held that Fleming had failed to prove the necessary *animus testandi* since one of the witnesses to Butterfield's testamentary intent knew that Butterfield had not really intended the instrument to be his will. The court allowed parol to contradict the statements contained in the instrument.

8. **Extrinsic Evidence Admissible to Ascertain Circumstances Under Which Will Was Made--**

Estate of Russell, 444 P.2d 353 (Cal. 1968).

Facts. The decedent, Thelma Russell, died leaving a validly executed holographic will written on a small card that bequeathed everything she owned to Chester Quinn, a close friend, and to Roxy Russell, her pet dog, which was alive on the date the will was executed but predeceased the testator. The reverse side of the card bequeathed a $10 gold piece and diamonds to Georgia Nan Russell Hembree (P), the niece and only heir at law of the testator. P brought a petition for determination of heirship, alleging that Roxy was a dog, that the Probate Code enumerates those entitled to take by will and that dogs are not included, that the gift of half of the estate to Roxy is void, and that P, as the testator's sole heir at law, is entitled to half of the residue. At the hearing, P introduced without objection extrinsic evidence that Roxy was the testator's dog. Quinn, through his attorney, introduced evidence of his relationship with the testator, and documentary evidence consisting of the testator's address book and a certain quitclaim deed, all of which was admitted over objection. The trial court held that it was the intention of the testator that Quinn was to receive her entire estate excepting the gold coin and diamonds bequeathed to P and that Quinn was to care for the dog in the event of the testator's death. The court held that the language in the will indicated that Quinn was to use whatever portion of the estate as might be necessary to care for and maintain the dog. P appeals.

Issue. May extrinsic evidence of the circumstances under which a will is made be considered in ascertaining what the testator meant by the words used in a will?

Held. Yes. Judgment reversed.

♦   When the language of a will is ambiguous or uncertain, resort may be had to extrinsic evidence in order to ascertain the intention of the testator. A latent ambiguity is one that is not apparent on the face of the will but is disclosed by some fact collateral to it, whereas a patent ambiguity is an uncertainty that appears on the face of the will. We think it is self-evident that in the interpretation of a will, a court cannot determine whether the terms of the will are clear and definite in the first place until it considers the circumstances under which the will was made. Extrinsic evidence of the circumstances under which a will is made may be considered by the court in ascertaining what the testator meant by the words used in the will.

♦   Here, extrinsic evidence offered by P to raise and resolve the latent ambiguity as to Roxy and to establish that Roxy was a dog was properly considered in order to ascertain what the testator meant by the words of the will. However, viewing the will in light of the surrounding circumstances, the trial court erred in holding that the testator intended to make an absolute gift of her entire estate to Quinn. A disposition in equal shares to two beneficiaries cannot be equated with a disposition of the whole to one of them, who may use whatever portion on behalf of the other. We conclude that the testator intended to make a disposition of all of the residue of the estate to Quinn and the dog in equal shares. As a dog cannot be the beneficiary under a will, the attempted gift to Roxy is void. Hence, that portion of the estate remains undisposed of by the will and passes to the heirs at law. We conclude that the residue of the estate should be distributed in equal shares to Quinn and P.

B.   DEATH OF BENEFICIARY BEFORE DEATH OF TESTATOR: LAPSE

When a beneficiary predeceases the testator, the beneficiary's bequest will lapse (and pass through the residuary estate or through intestacy) in the absence of an anti-lapse statute, which specifies substitute takers.

1. **UPC Section 2-601.** Under this section, if a devisee does not survive the testator by 120 hours, then he is treated as having predeceased the testator, unless the will contains some explicit language dealing specifically with simultaneous deaths.

2. **UPC Section 2-605.** Under this section, if a devisee who is a grandparent or a lineal descendant of a grandparent (i) is dead at the time of execution of the will, (ii) fails to survive the testator, or (iii) is treated as if he had predeceased the testator, then his issue who survive the testator by 120 hours take in his place. If the issue are all of the same degree of kinship to the devisee they take equally, but if they are of unequal degree then those of more remote degree take by representation.

3. **Anti-Lapse Statutes.** The states' anti-lapse statutes vary widely as to their scope. In many states, the anti-lapse statute applies only if the predeceasing beneficiary was a child or other descendant of the testator. Under the UPC and in several non-UPC states, the anti-lapse statute applies if the predeceasing beneficiary was a grandparent or a lineal descendant of a grandparent of the testator. In nearly all states, the anti-lapse statute operates only if the predeceasing beneficiary left descendants who survived the testator. Such descendants take the gift by substitution. In most states, the anti-lapse statute does not apply if the gift is contingent on the beneficiary's surviving the testator.

    a. **Anti-lapse statute does not apply--**

Allen v. Talley, 949 S.W.2d 59 (Tex. 1997).

Facts. At the time the decedent, Mary Shoults, executed her will, she had three brothers and two sisters alive. The will provided that all of her property was to be shared by her living brothers and sisters, whom she named. At the time of her death, only a brother and a sister were alive, but the deceased siblings all left children. Lewis Allen, Jr., a surviving child of one of the deceased brothers, filed an application for probate and issuance of letters of administration, as did the surviving sister, Lera Talley. The court admitted the will but did not appoint an administrator. After filing petitions for declaratory judgment, Lera argued that the language in the will operates as words of survivorship and precludes the application of the anti-lapse statute. Lewis argued that a class gift was not created and that the statute applies. Both parties filed motions for summary judgment; the trial court granted Lera's motion. Lewis appeals.

Issue. Does the decedent's will contain words of survivorship, which preclude application of the anti-lapse statute?

Held. Yes. Judgment affirmed.

♦   Since both parties agree that the language is not ambiguous, we construe the will based on the express language used.

♦ There were no other provisions in the will but that the decedent's living brothers and sisters take her whole estate, share and share alike. It is clear from the language that the decedent intended that her siblings who were living at the time of her death take her estate; otherwise, the phrase "share and share alike" followed by no other provisions would add nothing to the meaning of the will. Therefore, "living brothers and sisters" are words of survivorship.

Comments.

♦ A careful will drafter will provide for the contingency of the intended devisee not surviving the testator.

♦ The anti-lapse statutes do not operate to save a decedent's interest in property held in joint tenancy.

---

4. **Rule of Construction that "And" Be Read as "Or" to Effectuate Testator's Intent.** *Jackson v. Schultz*, 151 A.2d 284 (Del. 1959), involved the construction of a will to carry out the testator's intent. Leonard Bullock's will bequeathed all of his property to his wife, Bessie, "and of whatever nature and kind, to her and her heirs and assigns forever." Bessie had three children from a previous marriage, and she and Leonard had cared for them until they were adults. Leonard had no heirs, and Bessie predeceased him. When Leonard died, to avoid a lapse and an escheat to the state and to carry out Leonard's obvious testamentary purpose, the vice-chancellor determined that the "and" in Leonard's devise could be substituted by the word "or." Thus, the words "her heirs and assigns forever" were not words of limitation, defining the quantity of the estate devised, but they became words of substitution, designating those who would take if Bessie predeceased Leonard.

5. **Rule of Construction Held Inapplicable.** In *Hofing v. Willis*, 201 N.E.2d 852 (Ill. 1964), the court held that while there is some support for the proposition that the phrase "and to their heirs" could be considered as words of purchase by reading the word "and" as "or," the presence of the words "and assigns" makes such a construction unacceptable. The court stated that it is hardly reasonable to suppose that the grantor would create a substitutionary gift and at the same time designate the assigns of the named takers to take by way of substitution.

6. **No Class Gift--**

Dawson v. Yucus, 239 N.E.2d 305 (Ill. 1968).

Facts. Nelle Stewart's (T's) duly executed will devised her one-fifth interest in certain farmlands to two nephews, Wilson and Burtle, each taking one-half. Burtle died prior to T's death. Wilson filed suit to construe the will, alleging the devise was a class gift and that he, as survivor of the class, was entitled to the entire one-fifth interest. Wilson later conveyed the interest he allegedly received as survivor to Burtle's two children (Ps) and they were substituted as plaintiffs. The residuary beneficiaries (Ds) contend that the gift to Wilson and Burtle was not a class gift but instead a gift to two specific individuals. The trial court found for Ds. Ps appeal.

Issue. Was a class gift to the nephews created in T's will?

Held. No. Decree affirmed.

♦ A class gift is a gift of an aggregate sum to a body of persons uncertain in number at the time of the gift, to be ascertained at a future time, and who are all to take in equal or in some other definite proportions, the share of each being dependent for its amount upon the ultimate number of persons.

♦ Here, there were two named individuals, making certain the number of beneficiaries and their share. The shares do not depend upon the number who survive T.

♦ T used no class gift language, *i.e.,* "nephews," "cousins," "descendants," etc. and the will contained a survivorship gift of the residue of her estate; no survivorship gift was created in the clause devising the farmland.

---

7. **Gift to Class and Named Individual Who Predeceases the Testator.** *In re Moss,* [1899] 2 Ch. 314, *aff'd,* [1901] A.C. 187 (H.L.), Walter Moss had bequeathed his interest in the *Daily Telegraph* newspaper in trust to pay the income to his wife for life and, upon her death, in trust for E. J. Fowler (his niece) and his sister's children who attained the age of 21, to be divided equally among them as tenants in common. E.J. predeceased Moss, and it was argued that her share lapsed and this fell into the residue of the estate. However, the court held that a gift by will to a class and a named individual equally, so that the testator contemplates the individual taking the same share that each member of the class will take, is prima facie evidence of a gift to a class. Here, E.J. was only intended to share as one of a class, and because she did not survive, the rest of the class takes the whole of the property.

C. CHANGES IN PROPERTY AFTER EXECUTION OF WILL: SPECIFIC VS. GENERAL DEVISES

1. **Ademption.** If specifically devised property is not in the testator's estate at the time of death (*e.g.,* it was sold by the testator or destroyed), the gift is adeemed. This is known as ademption by extinction. The doctrine only applies to specific devises and bequests; general legacies are not affected.

   a. **Ademption by extinction--**

Wasserman v. Cohen, 606 N.E.2d 901 (Mass. 1993).

Facts. Frieda Drapkin created an inter vivos trust funded at execution, and retained the right to add property by inter vivos transfer and will and amend, revoke, and withdraw property from the trust. A trust provision ordered David Cohen (D), trustee, to convey a building to Elaine Wasserman (P). However, Drapkin had sold the building prior to her death and had never conveyed her interest in the property to the trust. P brought an action for declaratory judgment, requesting the trustee pay her the proceeds of the sale of the building. The probate judge dismissed the action. P applied for direct appellate review.

Issue. Does the doctrine of ademption by extinction apply to the specific gift of real estate contained in a revocable inter vivos trust?

Held. Yes. Judgment affirmed.

♦   When, during her lifetime, a testator disposes of the subject of a specific legacy in her will, that devise is held to be adeemed.

♦   A trust, particularly when executed as part of an estate plan, should be construed according to the same rules traditionally applied to wills.

---

2.   **Abatement.** Abatement is the process of reducing testamentary gifts in cases where the estate assets are not sufficient to pay all claims against the estate and satisfy all bequests and devises. At common law, all gifts of personal property abate before dispositions of real property. Today, in most states, the distinction between real and personal property has been abolished, and statutes provide a general order in which the types of gifts are abated.

    a.   **UPC section 2-608.** Under this section, a specific devisee has the right to a general pecuniary devise equal to the net sale price of devised property sold by a conservator.

3.   **Exoneration of Liens.** Most jurisdictions follow the doctrine of exoneration of liens, which presumes that specific dispositions of property subject to mortgages or other encumbrances are to be paid out of the testator's residuary estate, absent language to the contrary in the testator's will.

    a.   **UPC section 2-609: nonexoneration.** Under this section, property passes without the right of exoneration—a specific devise will pass *subject to* a security interest existing on the date of the testator's death, regardless of any provisions in the testator's will to pay the debt.

4.   **Satisfaction.** Satisfaction applies where a testator makes an inter vivos transfer to a beneficiary after executing a will, with the intention of making the testamentary

gift inoperative. At common law, a gift to a child of the testator is presumptively in partial or total satisfaction of any gifts made to the child in a previously executed will.

5. **Stock Splits.** Under the majority rule, a specific beneficiary is entitled to additional shares of stock produced by a stock split, but is not entitled to additional shares of stock produced by a stock dividend. Under the UPC, the specific beneficiary of corporate securities is entitled to additional or other securities of the same entity—*i.e.,* both stock splits and stock dividends.

VII. RESTRICTIONS ON THE POWER OF DISPOSITION: PROTECTION OF THE SPOUSE AND CHILDREN

A. RIGHTS OF THE SURVIVING SPOUSE

1. **Introduction to Marital Property Systems.** There are two basic marital property systems in the United States: (i) the common law system of separate property and (ii) the system of community property.

   a. **Separate property system.** Under this approach, each spouse is entitled to whatever property he earns—there is no sharing of earnings. This excludes jointly owned property.

      1) **Protection against disinheritance.** Nearly all of the common law jurisdictions have enacted elective share statutes designed to give the surviving spouse some protection against disinheritance. These statutes give the spouse an election to take a statutory share (usually one-third or one-half) of the decedent's estate in lieu of taking under the decedent's will.

   b. **Community property system.** Under this approach, any earnings, and property acquired from earnings, after marriage is owned in equal, undivided shares. In general, none of the community property states has an elective share statute. Each spouse has the power of testamentary disposition over only that spouse's one-half community interest. The surviving spouse automatically owns one-half of the community estate upon the other spouse's death.

2. **Rights of Surviving Spouse to Support.**

   a. **Social Security.** The surviving spouse is entitled to the decedent's Social Security benefits—the decedent may not transfer the benefits to anyone else. However, the surviving spouse may be required to share the benefits with the decedent's dependents.

   b. **Private pension plans.** ERISA requires that pensions paid under covered private pension plans must be paid as a joint and survivor annuity to the worker and the worker's spouse, unless the nonworker spouse consents to some other form of distribution of the retirement benefit.

   c. **Homestead.** Most states have statutes that secure some interest in the family home for the surviving spouse and minor children, free from claims of creditors. These homesteads are known as probate homesteads.

d. Personal property set-aside. Some statutes exempt certain items of tangible personal property from execution or levy in satisfaction of creditors' claims.

e. Family allowance. The surviving spouse or minor children are entitled to petition for a family allowance to provide for their maintenance during the period in which the decedent's estate is in administration.

f. Dower and curtesy. Dower was the provision the law made for a widow out of the husband's property. Upon the husband's death, the widow was entitled to a life estate in an undivided one-third of the husband's lands. A husband had a comparable interest in his wife's lands known as curtesy. Upon the wife's death, her husband's curtesy right gave him a life estate in all (not just an undivided one-third) of the lands of which the wife was seised during marriage. However, a husband's curtesy estate (unlike dower) arose only if issue were born to the marriage.

    1) Property subject to dower. Dower attaches to any land the husband owns at the time of the marriage and all subsequently acquired land. The husband cannot defeat the wife's dower interest by attempting a transfer of land without her joinder.

    2) Testamentary effect. Dower and curtesy rights could be asserted regardless of the decedent's will. Thus, a wife's dower interest in her husband's land was not affected by the fact that the husband had devised the land to another. To this extent, each spouse's power of testamentary disposition over property was limited by the other's dower or curtesy right.

    3) Present status of dower and curtesy. Most states have abolished dower and curtesy in favor of elective share statutes.

3. Rights of Surviving Spouse to a Share of Decedent's Property.

a. Elective share and its rationale. The majority of states give the surviving spouse an elective share of the deceased spouse's real and personal assets. The spouse can elect to either take under the deceased spouse's will or renounce the will and take a statutory share of the estate (usually one-third or one-half). Section 2-202(a) of the UPC provides a schedule to determine the elective share percentage determined by the length of the marriage. The surviving spouse is entitled to 50% of the decedent's estate after 15 years of marriage. In addition, if the surviving spouse's assets are less than $50,000, she is entitled to a supplemental elective share in the amount of $50,000.

b. Election required for public assistance--

***In re* Estate of Cross,** 664 N.E.2d 905 (Ohio 1996).

Facts. Carroll Cross died testate, leaving his estate to his son, Ray Cross (P), who was not the child of his surviving spouse, Beulah. Beulah, 80, suffered from Alzheimer's disease and was in a nursing home; her care was paid for by Medicaid. Pursuant to statute, the probate court appointed a commissioner who investigated the matter and concluded that the court should elect on Beulah's behalf to take against the estate. Beulah would then receive a spousal allowance of $25,000 and half of approximately $9,000. The probate court, after a hearing, so elected. P appealed. Beulah died while the appeal was pending. The appeals court reversed, finding that the election was not in Beulah's best interest and not necessary to provide for her support because her care was paid by Medicaid. Beulah's administrator (D) appeals and is joined by the board of commissioners that represented Beulah before the probate court.

Issue. Did the probate court judge abuse his discretion in electing for Beulah, who depended solely on Medicaid benefits for her support, to take against her deceased husband's will?

Held. No. Judgment reversed. Probate court judgment reinstated.

♦ The probate court has statutory authority to elect on behalf of a disabled spouse after ascertaining the spouse's adequate support needs and comparing the value of the spouse's share under the will with her rights under the statute of descent and distribution. The court must first consider other resources and the age, life expectancy, physical and mental condition, and anticipated future needs of the spouse and determine if the election is necessary to provide for her adequate support.

♦ The appeals court ignored Beulah's Medicaid eligibility requirements. Among the resources that are considered in determining eligibility for Medicaid is property devised to a recipient from a parent or spouse, including "those resources in which an applicant/recipient has a legal interest and the legal ability to use or dispose of . . . ." Medicaid rules state that an applicant or recipient who fails to use available income is ineligible for benefits.

♦ Here, to maintain Beulah's Medicaid eligibility and to continue to have her expenses provided by Medicaid, the judge was required to elect for Beulah to take against the will and receive her intestate share.

---

c. **No forced share in homosexual relationship--**

***In re* Estate of Cooper,** 592 N.Y.S.2d 797 (N.Y. App. Div. 1993).

Facts. Upon William Cooper's (T's) death, the bulk of his estate was left to his former lover, Ernest Chin (P). P, who had a homosexual relationship with T, petitioned the court to allow him to elect against the will. T's executrix (E) opposed and applied to dismiss P's action. The court found for E. P appeals.

Issue. Is a homosexual relationship a "spousal relationship" such that a survivor is entitled to a right of election against the decedent's will pursuant to the relevant statute?

Held. No. Decree affirmed.

♦ The statute permits a surviving spouse the right of election.

♦ A "surviving spouse" is defined as a husband or wife, but even if it were not, the language of a statute is generally construed according to its natural and most obvious sense in accord with its ordinary and accepted meaning.

♦ The traditional definition contemplates the survivor of a union between members of the opposite sex, and we see no reason to reject that.

♦ Any equal protection analysis in the instant case is to be measured by the rational basis standard, *i.e.,* the legislation is valid if the classification drawn is rationally related to a legitimate state interest.

♦ The Supreme Court of Minnesota rejected same sex petitioners' argument that a prohibition on same sex marriages denied them equal protection, holding: "the institution of marriage as a union of man and woman, uniquely involving the procreation and rearing of children within a family . . . [is] 'fundamental to the very existence and survival of the race.' This historic institution manifestly is more deeply founded than the asserted contemporary concept of marriage and societal interests for which petitioners contend." [Baker v. Nelson, 191 N.W.2d 185 (Minn. 1980)] The Supreme Court dismissed petitioners' appeal for want of a substantial federal question. "Such a dismissal is a holding that the constitutional challenge was considered and rejected." [Hicks v. Miranda, 422 U.S. 332 (1960)]

Comment. On appeal, the New York Court of Appeals dismissed on the ground that no substantial constitutional question was directly involved. [*In re* Cooper, 82 N.Y.2d 801, 624 N.E.2d 696, 604 N.Y.S.2d 558 (1993)]

---

    d.   **Surviving spouse's statutory share of assets of inter vivos trust created by deceased spouse--**

Sullivan v. Burkin, 460 N.E.2d 571 (Mass. 1984).

Facts. Mary Sullivan (P), a widow who exercised her statutory right to take a share of her husband's (Ernest's) estate, brought an action seeking determination that the assets held in inter vivos trust created by Ernest during marriage should be considered as part of the estate in determining that share. Ernest had executed a deed of trust under which he transferred real estate to himself as sole trustee. The net income of the trust was payable to him during his life and the trustee was instructed to pay to him all or such part of the principal of the trust estate as he might request in writing periodically. He retained the right to revoke the trust at any time. On his death, the successor trustee was directed to pay the principal and any undistributed income equally to George and Harold Cronin (Ds) if they should survive him, which they did. Ernest died while still trustee of the inter vivos trust. He left a will in which he stated that he intentionally neglected to make any provision for his wife and grandson. He directed that, after payment of debts, expenses, and all estate taxes levied by reason of his death, the residue of his estate should be paid over to the trustee of the inter vivos trust. The Probate Court rejected P's claim and entered judgment dismissing the complaint. Appeal was taken.

Issue. Are the assets of an inter vivos trust to be considered in determining the portion of the estate of the deceased to which a widow may claim her statutory share?

Held. No. Judgment affirmed.

- ◆ A trust with remainder interests given to others on the settlor's death is not invalid as a testamentary disposition simply because the settlor retained a broad power to modify or revoke the trust, the right to receive income, and the right to invade principal during his life.

- ◆ The fact that the settlor of a trust with remainder interests given to others on the settlor's death is the sole trustee does not make the trust testamentary.

- ◆ Whether or not the decedent established an inter vivos trust in order to defeat P's right to take her statutory share of the assets placed in trust, and even though the decedent had a general power of appointment over the trust assets, P obtained no right to share in the assets of that trust when she made her statutory election.

- ◆ In the future, as to any inter vivos trust created or amended after the date of this opinion, the estate of the decedent, for purposes of the surviving spouse's statutory share, shall include the value of assets held in an inter vivos trust created by the deceased spouse as to which he alone retained power during his life to direct disposition of those trust assets for his benefit, as, for example, by the exercise of a power of appointment or by revocation of the trust.

---

     e.   **Issue not resolved in *Sullivan*.** *Bongaards v. Millen*, 793 N.E.2d 335 (Mass. 2003), concerned questions left unanswered by the *Sullivan* decision, *supra*. Under the terms of a trust established by her mother, Jean Bongaards, the life tenant, had a limited power of appointment over the remainder.

During her life she could have terminated the trust, resulting in the entire trust corpus having been paid to her. Instead, Bongaards appointed the trust remainder to her sister. Because Bongaards had disinherited her husband in her will, he claimed an elective share against her estate. The court rejected his claim, noting that the trust was created, not by Bongaards, but by her mother, a third party. The court explained that the statutory language regarding elective shares concerns the division of the "estate of the deceased," which means the decedent's probate estate. The court declined to expand the term, despite the myriad of will substitutes available, since it would be up to the legislature to do so. While *Sullivan* may appear to represent a tinkering with the definition of "estate," it simply closed a loophole by means of which spouses could evade the statutory definition. *Sullivan* kept in the elective share "estate" property the decedent had owned, which would have been in the estate absent an attempt to remove the property while still retaining access to it via a trust. In *Bongaards*, the property was never in the estate in the first place.

1) **State statutes.** Many states have enacted statutes to provide criteria for determining what nonprobate transfers are subject to the elective share. Delaware, for example, includes property that would be included in the decedent's gross estate under federal estate tax law.

f. **UPC right to elective share.** Under the UPC, the surviving spouse has a right to a percentage of the decedent's "augmented estate" based on the length of the marriage. UPC section 2-203 combines the properties to be included in the augmented estate. Nonprobate assets—such as life insurance policies, pension plans, bonds, and bank accounts—frequently pass to beneficiaries outside of the will. As a result, instances arise where the surviving spouse may receive too great a share of the decedent's estate, or too little. Under the UPC, the spouse's share from the augmented estate includes the following:

1) The probate estate less funeral expenses, claims, and various family allowances;

2) The value of property transferred during the marriage without the consent of the spouse by arrangements that are, in effect, will substitutes;

3) Property acquired by the surviving spouse from the decedent or otherwise transferred to the surviving spouse;

4) The value of the surviving spouses's property and nonprobate transfers to others that would have been in her augmented estate upon her death; and

5) Life insurance proceeds payable to any person other than the surviving spouse.

g.   **Source of elective share.** Statutes in some states provide that values included in the augmented estate that pass or have passed to the surviving spouse are applied first to satisfy the elective share and to reduce any contributions due from other recipients of transfers included in the augmented estate.

h.   **Other statutes.** New York provides generously for a surviving spouse. Its elective share statutes provide that the surviving spouse is entitled to the entire estate if it is in the $100,000 range. In addition to the probate estate, the following will substitutes are subject to the elective share: (i) gifts causa mortis; (ii) savings account trusts; (iii) contributions to joint bank accounts; (iv) property payable on death to a person other than the decedent; and (v) revocable lifetime transfers, pension plans, and property over which the decedent had a general power of appointment. The elective share is reduced by the value of any interest (other than a life estate) that passes from the decedent to the surviving spouse. In contrast, Delaware includes in the elective share all property includible in the gross estate for federal estate tax purposes, regardless of whether the decedent files an estate tax return.

i.   **Waiver.** A surviving spouse may voluntarily waive his rights to election, homestead allowance, exempt property, or family allowance by a written and executed agreement.

1)   **Waiver upheld--**

In re **Estate of Garbade,** 633 N.Y.S. 2d 878 (1995).

Facts. In 1990, Respondent (R) married J. Robert Garbade, the decedent, a wealthy executive, after signing a prenuptial agreement in which R waived her elective share, among other provisions. The agreement also required the decedent to maintain a $100,000 policy on his life for R's benefit. Following the decedent's unexpected death in 1992, R received assets totaling approximately $340,000 and filed notice of her election to take her share of the decedent's estate. The decedent's sons from a previous marriage, Petitioners (Ps), moved for summary judgment, claiming R's right had been waived. R claimed the waiver had been procured by fraud, misrepresentation, and duress. The court entered judgment for Ps. R appeals.

Issue. Was the prenuptial agreement procured by fraud?

Held. No. Judgment affirmed.

♦   Like any other contract, a duly executed prenuptial agreement is given a presumption of legality. The party attacking the agreement's validity has the burden of proving fraud.

♦   R presented evidence to show that it was the decedent who had first raised the issue of an agreement and asked that it be executed before the wedding. The decedent's lawyer had prepared the agreement and it was signed only a few hours before the wedding. R did not obtain legal counsel, nor did she read the agreement before signing it. R was not told of the provision waiving her elective share and was not provided with a copy of the agreement.

♦ However, it was uncontroverted that R readily agreed to the agreement because she did not want the decedent's money; she just wanted to be his wife. Prior to signing, R was told the full scope of the decedent's wealth, was advised to obtain counsel, and was given the opportunity to read the agreement.

♦ There is no evidence of fraud here. R has established only that she was derelict in not reading the agreement and in not consulting counsel.

––––––––––––––––––

4. **Rights of Surviving Spouse in Community Property.**

   a. **Introduction.** In all of the community property states, if an intestate is not survived by descendants, the intestate's one-half share of the community estate passes to the surviving spouse. Because the other half of the community estate belongs to the surviving spouse, the surviving spouse succeeds to the entire estate. In several states, the surviving spouse takes the entire community estate even if the decedent was survived by descendants. In others, the decedent's one-half community share is inherited by his descendants.

   b. **Classification of assets as community or separate property.** This classification is important for tax reasons since under federal tax law the entire value of a spouse's separate property but only one-half of the community property is included in the deceased spouse's gross estate.

   c. **Putting the survivor to an election.** Under the widow's election, an estate planning device, the deceased spouse's will purports to dispose of the entire community property and not just an undivided one-half share, giving the surviving spouse an election, such that if the surviving spouse lays claim to her community interest, she loses the testamentary gifts in her favor. On the other hand, if the testator disposes only of his separate property and his one-half share of community property, the surviving spouse may claim both her share of community property and her devise under the will.

5. **Migrating Couples and Multistate Property Holdings.**

   a. **Migration from separate property state to community property state.** When a couple moves from a separate property state to a community property state, potential problems arise in determining what the surviving spouse is entitled to upon her husband's death, particularly if he earned or acquired the majority of their property while domiciled in the separate property state. This occurs because ownership of property is determined in accordance with the laws of the state in which the couple was domiciled when it was acquired or earned. Two states, California and Idaho, give the surviving spouse a remedy in these situations through the concept of quasi-community property. Quasi-community property is property acquired by one spouse while domiciled in another state that would have been classified as community property had it been acquired while the spouse was domiciled in the community property state. Real property located in another state does not constitute quasi-community property. When the acquiring spouse dies, one-half of the quasi-community property goes to the surviving spouse and the other half is disposed of according to the decedent's will. The non-acquiring spouse has no testamentary powers over the quasi-community property if she dies first—the entire property belongs to the acquiring spouse.

b. **Migration from community property state to separate property state.** In general, such a change does not affect the rights of the husband or wife. Community property retains its status as community property when the couple and the property move to a separate property state.

c. **Uniform Disposition of Community Property Rights at Death Act.** Under this Act, one-half of the property to which the Act applies is the property of the surviving spouse and is not subject to testamentary disposition by the decedent. This Act has been adopted in about a dozen states.

6. **Spouse Omitted from Premarital Will.**

a. **States without statutes.** The states are divided on the effect of marriage on a previously executed will. In about half the states, marriage by itself does not affect the will. *Rationale:* The new spouse is given adequate protection by dower or elective share statutes (or, in a community property state, by the community property system).

b. **Statutory solutions.** About half the states have statutes under which the testator's subsequent marriage has an effect on the will. In most of these states, the will is only partially revoked. The marriage revokes the will only to the extent of providing the new spouse with an intestate share. After distribution of the spouse's intestate share, the will operates to distribute the remaining assets. These are sometimes referred to as "pretermitted spouse" statutes. Note that the above statutes often provide that the will is not partially or totally revoked if (i) there has been provision for the new spouse outside the will and in lieu of a testamentary provision, (ii) the will provides that the spouse's omission was intentional, or (iii) it appears that the will was made in contemplation of marriage.

c. **Spouse omitted from premarital will--**

Estate of Shannon, 274 Cal. Rptr. 338 (1990).

Facts. Russell Shannon (T) executed his will in 1974, naming his daughter sole beneficiary and executrix. T married in 1986 and died in 1988; T made no changes in his will, which was admitted to probate. T's wife Lila (P) petitioned the probate court to determine heirship. The petition was denied. P appeals. During the pendency of the appeal, P died and her son was substituted as appellant.

Issue. Was P a pretermitted spouse?

Held. Yes. Order reversed and case remanded.

♦ The relevant statute provides that if a testator fails to provide in his will for a surviving spouse who married the testator after the execution of the testator's will, the omitted spouse shall receive a share.

♦ None of the exceptions that would preclude P from sharing in T's estate apply. T's failure to provide for P does not appear from the will to be intentional. No evidence shows T provided for P outside the will. P did not execute an agreement to waive her share.

♦ The exclusionary clause, without more, is insufficient to avoid the statutory presumption of revocation of the will as to the omitted spouse based on public policy.

B. RIGHTS OF ISSUE OMITTED FROM THE WILL

Pretermitted child statutes are designed to protect children who have been accidentally omitted from the will. In most states, the statute operates only in favor of children born or adopted after the will's execution. In other states, the pretermitted child statute applies to children alive when the will was executed as well as to afterborn and after-adopted children.

1. In Australia--

Lambeff v. Farmers Co-operative Executors & Trustees Ltd., 56 S.A.S.R. 323 (Australia 1991).

Facts. In 1945, George Lambeff (T) married and had a child (P). T and his first wife separated in 1956. A short time later, T began seeing his second wife and had two sons with her. At the time of T's death, P was earning $33,000 per year and had purchased a flat that was valued at $120,000 and carried a mortgage of $66,000. Other than clothes, furniture, and jewelry, P had no assets, was unmarried, and had no children. P claimed in an affidavit that she attempted to reestablish contact with T on three occasions at five-year intervals, but T never responded. When T died, his older son (D1) was 33, married, and expecting a third child. He had worked with his father since he was 10 and claimed that he was always underpaid. He said that he continued to help T until his death because T promised him a caravan park, the largest estate asset, where D1 and his family lived. D1 and his wife managed the park since 1980 and relied on the income earned from it and from other contract work. His assets totaled $27,500. The younger son (D2) was 30 and had a de facto wife and two children. He failed his fourth year of high school and worked for his father in the caravan park. D2 and his family lived rent-free in a house owned by his mother, and his assets totaled $30,350. T made provision in his 1988 will for his whole estate to be held upon trust for his two sons in equal shares. P claims that she was left without adequate provision for her proper advancement in life.

Issue. If a person who is entitled to claim the benefit of the Inheritance (Family Provision) Act is left, through testamentary dispositions, without adequate provision for her proper advancement in life, may the court order that such provision be made out of the deceased's estate?

Held. Yes.

♦ The act provides that where a person domiciled in the state or owning real or personal property in the state dies without leaving adequate provision for the "proper" maintenance, education, or advancement in life for a person entitled by reason of the laws of intestacy or testamentary dispositions to claim the benefit of the act, the court may order such provision.

♦ The word "proper" means proper in all of the circumstances of the case, including the size of the estate, the needs of the applicants, the relationships with the deceased, and any special or competing claims.

♦ The court must place itself in the position of the testator and consider what he would have done if he had been wise and just.

♦ P is better off than the sons, but the sons are both young and healthy. P was abandoned at 10 and had no support from her father thereafter. She is to be paid a legacy of $20,000 from the estate.

---

2.   **Child Born After Will But Before Codicil--**

Azcunce v. Estate of Azcune, 586 So. 2d 1216 (Fla. 1991).

Facts. René Azcunce (T) executed a will that established a trust for the benefit of his spouse and his then-born children; there was no provision for after-born children. T subsequently executed a codicil that republished the terms of the will. T's daughter, Patricia (P), was born after this first codicil but before a second, which, again, republished the will and first codicil and made no mention of after-born children. T died of a heart attack at age 38. P petitioned for a statutory share as a pretermitted child. The trial court denied the petition. P appeals.

Issue. May a child who is born after the execution of her father's will, but before the execution of a codicil to the will, take a statutory share under Florida's pretermitted child statute when the will and codicil fail to provide for the child and all the other statutory requirements for pretermitted child status are otherwise satisfied?

Held. No. Order affirmed.

♦ Under the statute, prior to the second codicil, P was a pretermitted child, a child born after the making of the will who had not received a portion of T's property by way of advancement.

♦ The second codicil expressly stated that it republished the original will and first codicil. Thus, P's pretermitted status was destroyed.

♦ If T had wished to provide for P, presumably, he would have done so in the second codicil. P was, in effect, disinherited.

♦ There is no ambiguity in the will and codicils that would authorize the taking of parole evidence.

———————

a. **Aftermath—no malpractice suit without priority.** In *Espinosa v. Sparber, Shevin, Shapo, Rosen & Heilbronner*, 612 So. 2d 1378 (Fla. 1993), the court held that Patricia did not have standing to sue her father's attorney for malpractice, because she was not in privity with the attorney and she was not an intended third-party beneficiary. The court did not allow extrinsic evidence to explain the testator's intent, due to the risk of misinterpretation. However, the court held that the testator's estate stood in his shoes, and this satisfied the privity requirement.

3. **Great-Grandchildren Not Pretermitted Heirs--**

———————

In re Estate of Laura, 690 A.2d 1011 (N.H. 1997).

———————

Facts. Edward Laura (T) executed a will in 1984 and subsequently died in 1990. The will provided that T's estate would pass to his daughter, Shirley, and specifically disinherited his son Edward and his two grandchildren, Richard and Neil, children of his deceased daughter, Jo Ann. After the will was executed, Neil had two children, Cecilia and Neil III

(T's great-grandchildren). Prior to his death in 1990, T attempted to execute a codicil to the 1984 will that would have divided his estate in proportionate shares between Shirley and her children, Edward and his children, and Richard. However, the codicil was not properly witnessed, and upon T's death, the 1984 will was offered and accepted for probate. Richard and T's great-grandchildren (Ps) challenge the will and claim they are pretermitted heirs. The probate court adopted the master's findings that Ps were not pretermitted heirs. Ps appeal.

Issue. Are Ps pretermitted heirs under the relevant statute?

Held. No. Judgment affirmed.

♦ The relevant statute states: "Every child born after the decease of the testator, and every child or issue of a child of the deceased not named or referred to in his will, and who is not a devisee or legatee, shall be entitled to the same portion of the estate, real and personal, as he would be if the deceased were intestate."

♦ The statute protects against the omission of a child unless that omission is shown in the will to be intentional.

♦ While Cecilia and Neil III were not named in T's will, their father was specifically disinherited. Where a testator has specifically named an heir to disinherit him, he has referred to the heir's issue for the purpose of the statute.

♦ If a testator's child is mentioned in his will, that child's issue are not pretermitted heirs. Here, T's will specifically names his predeceased daughter, Jo Ann. Thus, her issue, Ps, are not pretermitted heirs.

VIII. TRUSTS: CREATION AND CHARACTERISTICS

A. INTRODUCTION

1. **Background.** The trustee of a trust owns the legal interest of the trust property while the beneficiary owns the equitable interest.

2. **The Settlor.** The settlor is the person who creates the trust. A trust created during the settlor's lifetime is an inter vivos trust. A trust created in the settlor's will is a testamentary trust.

3. **The Trustee.** The trustee may be a third party or a beneficiary. Failure to name a trustee will not defeat a trust; a court will appoint a trustee.

4. **The Beneficiaries.** Beneficiaries hold equitable interests. They have a personal claim against the trustee for breach of trust, and equitable claims on the trust property itself.

5. **Use of Trusts in Estate Planning.** Trusts can be used to avoid the probate process. Also, trusts can be used to secure certain tax advantages and for property management, including transferring property to minors or incompetents.

6. **A Trust Compared with a Legal Life Estate.** In most cases, creating a trust with the donee as life beneficiary is preferable to giving the donee a legal life estate, since resolution of various administrative problems with the estate is facilitated by having a trustee.

B. CREATION OF A TRUST

1. **Intent to Create a Trust.** While the settlor must have the intent to create a trust, no particular words need to be used. It is sufficient for the grantor to convey property to a grantee to hold for the use and benefit of another.

   a. **Need not expressly direct that subject matter be held in trust--**

Jimenez v. Lee, 547 P.2d 126 (Or. 1976).

Facts. In 1945, the paternal grandmother of Betsy Lee Jimenez (P) purchased a $1,000 United States Savings Bond registered in the name of P and/or Jason Lee (D), the father of P, and/or Dorothy Lee, the mother of P, to be used for P's educational needs. In 1956, Mrs. Adolph Diercks gave $500 to P and made identical gifts to D's other two children. Mrs. Diercks deposited the $1,500 in a savings account in the names of D and his three children.

Thereafter, D cashed the savings bond and invested the proceeds in common stock of the Commercial Bank of Salem, Oregon, with the shares registered as "Jason Lee, Custodian . . . for Betsy Lee [P]." At the same time, D closed the joint savings account and invested $1,000 of the proceeds in Commercial Bank stock, taking this stock as custodian for his children. P contends that the gifts for her educational needs created trusts in each instance and that the trusts survived D's investment of the trust assets in the Commercial Bank stock. P brought an action for an accounting. The trial court held for D. P appeals.

Issues.

(i)   To create a trust relationship, is it essential to expressly direct that the subject matter of a gift be held in trust?

(ii)   Does a trustee have the responsibility to administer a trust solely in the interest of the beneficiary of the trust and to prove that any expenditures made were made for trust purposes?

Held. (i) No. (ii) Yes. Case reversed and remanded.

♦   It is undisputed that the gifts were made for the educational needs of P. While the respective donors did not expressly direct D to hold the subject matter of the gift in trust, this is not essential to create a trust relationship. It is enough if the transfer of the property is made with the intent to vest the beneficial ownership in a third person. This was clearly shown in the present case.

♦   Having decided that a trust was created for the benefit of P, it follows that D's purchase of the Commercial Bank stock as custodian for P was ineffectual to expand D's powers over the trust property from that of trustee to that of custodian. D's attempt to broaden his power violated his duty to the beneficiary to administer the trust solely in the interest of the beneficiary. Here, many of the items that D lists as trust expenditures are either questionable or clearly outside the purpose of an educational trust. The trial court therefore erred in finding that P has received the accounting that she sought and is entitled to no further accounting.

♦   The case must be remanded for an accounting to be predicated upon a trustee's duty to account and the trustee's burden to prove that the expenditures were made for trust purposes. In determining whether D has met this strict burden of proof, the trial court must adhere to the rule that all doubts are resolved against a trustee who maintains an inadequate accounting system.

---

     b.   Custodianship Under Uniform Transfers to Minors Act. Under this Act, a gift to a minor may be transferred to a person as custodian for the benefit of the minor. The creation of this custodianship is simpler than the creation of a trust. The custodian is a fiduciary. To the extent that the custodial property is not expended for the minor's benefit, the custodian is required to transfer the property to the minor on his attaining the age of 21 or, if the minor dies before attaining the age of 21, to the estate of the minor.

c. **Precatory language and equitable charges.** Precatory language—such as "To A with the hope that A will care for B"—creates a moral obligation unenforceable at law. Uncertainty can be avoided by specifying that only a moral obligation is desired; *e.g.,* "I wish, but do not legally require, that A will care for B." Likewise, an equitable charge (not a trust) occurs when a testator devises property to a person provided that person pays a certain sum of money to another person.

d. **No intention to impose trustee duties--**

The Hebrew University Association v. Nye (Hebrew University Association I), 169 A.2d 641 (Conn. 1961).

Facts. Hebrew University (P) obtained a judgment declaring it was the owner of a rare book collection purchased by Professor Yahuda and his wife Ethel during the professor's lifetime. Ethel had purchased a part of the collection inventoried in the professor's estate when he died, and at her death, she owned the complete collection. Professor Yahuda and Ethel had indicated to friends before the professor's death that both wished to create a scholarship research center in Israel. Professor Yahuda had forwarded some of the books to New Haven for shipment overseas, but no consignee was named and the books remained in New Haven and were purchased by Ethel at the professor's death. Thereafter, Ethel visited P in Israel and announced her gift at a luncheon. The next day, Ethel signed a press release prepared by P, indicating Ethel had made a gift to P. Ethel also provided P with a memorandum listing most of the library's contents, and its important books and documents. [*See* Hebrew University Association II, *infra*] Later, Ethel stated orally and in writing that she "had given" the library to P, she refused offers of purchase, and told others the library did not belong to her. Ethel crated and catalogued the books, and up to the time of her death, corresponded with P about delivering the library, and sent some items to a warehouse for delivery. Upon Ethel's death, P sought a declaratory judgment determining whether P or Nye (D), Ethel's estate's representative, owned the library, but P's complaint contained no theory based upon which ownership was claimed. D appeals.

Issue. Is P the owner of the library?

Held. No. Case remanded for a new trial.

♦ The judgment below provided no basis for the court's conclusion that a trust was created at the luncheon when Ethel made public her intention to create the trust.

♦ The facts indicate that Ethel intended, and possibly attempted, to give an executed, present, legal inter vivos gift to P without delivery.

♦ Because a gift fails for lack of delivery, the intent to give cannot be carried into effect through the presumption that the donor intended to have made herself trustee to make the necessary delivery.

♦ One may constitute herself trustee of personal property and create a trust enforceable in equity, even without consideration or delivery. However, while the term "trustee" does not have to be used, the donor must show an intent to impose upon herself enforceable duties of a trustee.

♦ No facts are provided in the opinion below indicating that Ethel ever imposed trustee duties on herself.

---

e.   **Constructive delivery--**

The Hebrew University Association v. Nye (Hebrew University Association II), 223 A.2d 397 (Conn. 1966).

Facts. *See* Hebrew University Association I, *supra.*

Issue. Is P the legal and equitable owner of the library with the right to immediate possession of its contents?

Held. Yes. Judgment entered for P.

♦ P claims constructive delivery by means of Ethel's memorandum. Constructive delivery requires delivery as nearly perfect and complete as the type of property and the circumstances will permit. Constructive delivery has been found in delivery of keys, pointing out hiding places, and an informal memorandum.

♦ Here, delivery of the memorandum, along with Ethel's acts and declarations that clearly show her intention to give a gift and to divest herself of ownership, was sufficient to complete the gift.

---

2.   **Necessity of Trust Property.** A trust must have trust property. Any type of property—contingent remainders, life insurance policies, leasehold interests—will suffice. The main concern is whether the particular claim will be deemed property by a court.

a.   **Promise to make gifts in the future--**

Unthank v. Rippstein, 386 S.W.2d 134 (Tex. 1964).

Facts. C.P. Craft wrote a letter to Iva Rippstein (P), promising to pay her $200 a month for the next five years provided he lived that long. In the margin of the letter, he wrote: "I have stricken out the words 'provided I live that long' and hereby and herewith bind my estate to make the $200 monthly payments." Craft died three days after writing the letter. P brought suit against the executors of his estate (Ds) for declaratory judgment adjudicating their liability to pay future installments as they matured. The trial court granted the executors' motion for summary judgment. The court of appeals reversed and rendered judgment for P, holding that the writing in question established a voluntary trust under which Craft bound his property to the extent of the promised payments. Ds appeal.

Issue. Is a writing promising to make gifts in the future binding as a voluntary trust?

Held. No. The judgment of the court of appeals is reversed and that of the trial court is affirmed.

♦ While the transactions under review are in the form of voluntary trusts, they are governed in general by the rules applicable to gifts. The principal difference between such a trust and a gift lies in the fact that in the case of a gift the thing given passes to the donee, while in the case of a voluntary trust only the equitable or beneficial title passes to the beneficiary.

♦ Here, the language of the notation of Craft cannot be expanded to show an intention on the part of Craft to place his property in trust. The most Craft did was to express an intention to make monthly gifts to P accompanied by an ineffectual attempt to bind his estate in futuro; the writing was no more than a promise to make similar gifts in the future and as such is unenforceable.

---

b. **Resulting and constructive trusts.**

1) **Resulting trust.** Resulting trusts arise by operation of law when (i) an express trust fails or (ii) a person pays the purchase price for property but title results in the name of another person who is not related to the purchaser (purchase money resulting trust).

2) **Constructive trust.** Constructive trusts are flexible remedies imposed to prevent unjust enrichment. The trustee must convey the property to the wronged party. Requirements for a constructive trust are:

(i) A confidential relationship;

(ii) A transferee's promise, express or implied;

(iii) A transfer of property in reliance on the promise; and

(iv) Unjust enrichment of the transferee.

A constructive trust may also be imposed to avoid unjust enrichment. A promise or confidential relationship need not exist.

c. **Trust distinguished from debt.** The crucial factor to differentiate between a trust relationship and an ordinary debt is whether the recipient of the funds is entitled to use them as his own and commingle them with his own monies.

1) **Trust based on interest not in existence.** *Brainard v. Commissioner*, 91 F.2d 880 (7th Cir. 1937), involved the question of whether a taxpayer's declaration created a valid trust over future profits. Brainard had stated to his wife and mother that he declared a trust of his stock trading for the benefit of his family. He agreed to assume personally any losses resulting from the venture and to distribute the profits, if any, in equal shares to his wife, mother, and two children after deducting reasonable compensation for his services. Brainard carried on his trading operations, and at the end of the year, determined his compensation to be slightly less than $10,000, which he reported in his income tax for that year. The profits remaining were then divided among the members of the family in approximately equal shares, which they reported in their respective income tax returns. The court held that a trust cannot be based on an interest that had not come into existence at the time the trust was declared because there was no res at that time. If there was no res at the time of the declaration, the settlor must manifest his intent to create a trust when the res comes into existence. Until that time, Brainard was the sole owner of the profits, and the profits were properly taxed to him as part of his income.

2) **Gift made of property not in existence at time of gift--**

Speelman v. Pascal, 178 N.E.2d 723 (N.Y. 1961).

Facts. In 1952, Gabriel Pascal Enterprises, Ltd. made an agreement with the estate of George Bernard Shaw that granted to the corporation the exclusive rights to prepare and produce a musical play based on Shaw's *Pygmalion* and a motion picture version of the musical. Prior to this agreement, Pascal had produced a nonmusical movie version of the play under rights obtained by Pascal from Shaw during Shaw's life. The new agreement provided that the Shaw estate would receive 3% of the receipts of the musical play and movie. It also provided that the license was to terminate if the licensee did not arrange to have the play produced within certain time periods. At a time when the license still had two years to run, Gabriel Pascal, who died shortly thereafter, wrote, signed, and delivered to Speelman (P) a letter that confirmed that he would give to P 5% of the profits obtained in

England and throughout the world and 2% of the profits in the United States. P brought suit to enforce Pascal's promise to pay the share of the profits. The trial court held for P. Mrs. Pascal (D), Pascal's widow, appeals.

Issue. May a valid present gift be made of property that is not in existence at the time the gift is made?

Held. Yes. Judgment affirmed.

♦ The question here is: Did the delivery of the letter constitute a valid, complete, present gift to P by way of assignment of a share in future royalties? We hold that it did. There are many instances of courts enforcing assignments of rights to sums that were expected thereafter to become due to the assignor. In those cases that failed, there had not been such a completed and irrevocable delivery of the subject matter of the gift as to put the gift beyond cancellation by the donor. Here, there was nothing left for Pascal to do to make an irrevocable transfer to P of part of Pascal's right to receive royalties from the productions.

---

3. **Necessity of Trust Beneficiaries.** A trust must have a beneficiary. However, the beneficiary may be unborn or unascertained when the trust is created. If there is more than one beneficiary and they are too indefinite to be ascertained at the time the trust becomes effective, the trust may fail, in which case there will be a resulting trust in favor of the settlor, his heirs, or other successors in interest.

   a. **Identification of beneficiaries--**

Clark v. Campbell, 133 A. 166 (N.H. 1926).

Facts. The will of the decedent bequeathed to his trustees articles of personal property "such as books, photographic albums, pictures, statuary, [etc.]" to give to the decedent's friends as the trustees shall select. The lower court reserved the question of whether the enumeration of the chattels was intended to be restrictive or merely indicative of the variety of personal property bequeathed. On appeal, it is argued that the bequest for the benefit of the testator's friends must fail for want of certainty of beneficiaries.

Issues.

(i) Does a bequest to a trustee to distribute personal property to a testator's friends constitute a private trust?

(ii) Must a private trust have a beneficiary or a class of beneficiaries indicated in the will capable of coming into court and claiming the benefit of the bequest?

Held. (i) Yes. (ii) Yes. Case discharged.

♦ At common law, there cannot be a bequest to an indefinite person. There must be a beneficiary or a class of beneficiaries indicated in the will capable of coming into court and claiming the benefit of the bequest. This principle applies to private trusts but not to public trusts and charities. Here, the language of the will, granting the trustees property of the described class to give to the testator's friends as they shall select, clearly discloses an intention to create a private trust.

♦ However, we hold that the will does not provide for definite and ascertainable beneficiaries. Thus, it cannot be sustained as a private trust. The word "friends," unlike "relations," has no accepted statutory or other controlling limitations and in fact has no precise sense at all. No sufficient criterion is furnished to govern the selection of the individuals from the class.

♦ When a gift is impressed with a trust ineffectively declared and incapable of taking effect because of the indefiniteness of the beneficiary, the donee will hold the property in trust for the next taker under the will, or for the next of kin by way of a resulting trust. The trustees therefore hold the property under consideration to be disposed of as part of the residue.

---

b. **Honorary trusts--**

In re **Searight's Estate,** 95 N.E.2d 779 (Ohio 1950).

Facts. The will of the decedent, George Searight, bequeathed his dog, Trixie, to Florence Hand, and directed his executor to deposit $1,000 to be used by him to pay Hand the sum of 75¢ per day for the care of the dog as long as it shall live. Hand accepted the bequest of Trixie and the executor paid her 75¢ per day for the keep and care of the dog. The trial court held the provision in the will valid. This appeal followed.

Issues.

(i) Is the creation of a trust for the benefit of a specific animal the proper subject of an honorary trust?

(ii) Does a bequest for the benefit of a specific animal "as long as it shall live" violate the Rule Against Perpetuities?

Held. (i) Yes. (ii) No. Judgment affirmed.

♦ A bequest for the care of a specific animal is an "honorary trust," that is, one binding the conscience of the trustee, since there is no beneficiary capable of enforcing the trust. The modern authorities uphold the validity of such gifts where the person to whom the power is given is willing to carry out the testator's wishes. We hold that the bequest for the care of the dog, Trixie, is not in and of itself unlawful.

♦ Nor does the bequest violate the Rule Against Perpetuities. It is to be noted that unless a trust established for specific animals limits the duration of the trust—that is, the time during which the power is to be exercised—to human lives, we will have honorary trusts established for animals of great longevity that possibly could continue longer than the maximum period allowed by the Rule Against Perpetuities. Here, however, the rule is not violated since the money given for the purpose of caring for the animal is limited to $1,000 at 75¢ per day. This sum of money will be fully exhausted in three years and 238 1/3 days. It is thus apparent that the testator provided a time limit for the exercise of the power given to the executor and that such time limit is less than the maximum period allowed under the Rule Against Perpetuities.

---

4. **Oral Inter Vivos Trusts of Land.** An oral inter vivos trust of personal property is enforceable, but if the subject matter of the oral trust is land, a written instrument is required to make the trust effective. However, some courts will impose a constructive trust upon property if the transferee stood in a confidential relationship to the transferor.

   a. **Oral promise to reconvey land held sufficient to impose a constructive trust.** In *Hieble v. Hieble*, 316 A.2d 777 (Conn. 1972), Mrs. Hieble had transferred title of her real estate by deed to her son and to her daughter. The motivation for the transfer was that Mrs. Hieble feared a recurrence of cancer and wanted to avoid probate. She and the grantees orally agreed that the transfer would be temporary, that she would remain in control of the property and pay all expenses and taxes, and that once the illness had passed, the grantees would reconvey the property to her upon request. Five years after the conveyance, Mrs. Hieble requested that her son reconvey his title to her. He refused, and she brought suit against him, seeking a reconveyance of the property. The court found that the parties stood in a confidential relationship and that although the bond between parent and child is not per se a fiduciary one, it does generate a natural inclination to repose great confidence and trust. When the owner of an interest in land transfers it inter vivos to another, in trust for the transferor, and the transferee orally promises to reconvey it at a later time but subsequently refuses to do so, the transferee holds the interest in a constructive trust for the transferor if at the time of the transfer they were in a confidential relationship.

5. **Oral Trusts for Disposition at Death.** If a testator devises property to his executors in a trust not defined in the will, but the existence of which the testator has communicated to the executors before the will's execution, some courts hold that the trust may be proved by oral evidence. Other courts refuse to follow this

line of decisions, holding that the trust has not been sufficiently defined by the will to take effect, and the equitable interest goes by way of resulting trust to the heirs as property of the deceased.

a. Trusts not sufficiently defined--

Olliffe v. Wells, 130 Mass. 221 (1881).

Facts. The will of the decedent, Ellen Donovan, left the residue of her estate to Rev. Wells (D) to distribute in such manner as in his discretion shall appear best calculated to carry out the wishes that she had expressed to him or may express to him. The heirs of the decedent (Ps) brought suit against D, claiming that the residue should be distributed to them. In his answer, D stated that the decedent had stated to him her wish that her estate be used for charitable purposes. D further stated that he desired and intended to distribute the residue for these purposes.

Issue. If a will shows the devisee to take legal title only and not the beneficial interest, and the trust is not sufficiently defined by will to take effect, will a court impose a resulting trust on the heirs of the decedent as to the property of the decedent not disposed of by will?

Held. Yes. Judgment for Ps.

♦　　It has been held that if a testator devises property to his executors in trusts not defined in the will, but which, as he states in the will, he has communicated to them before the will's execution, the trusts, if for lawful purposes, may be proved by the admission of the executors or by oral evidence and enforced against them. It has also been held that the trusts may be enforced against the heirs or next of kin.

♦　　We reject this line of cases. The will on its face shows that the devisee takes the legal title only and not the beneficial interest, and the trust is not sufficiently defined by the will to take effect. Thus, the equitable interest goes, by way of resulting trust, to the heirs as property of the deceased, not disposed of by will. They cannot be deprived of that equitable interest unless signified in those forms that the law makes essential to every testamentary disposition. A trust not sufficiently declared on the face of the will cannot therefore be set up by extrinsic evidence to defeat the rights of the heirs at law.

C. RIGHTS OF THE BENEFICIARIES TO DISTRIBUTIONS FROM THE TRUST

In a ***mandatory trust***, the trustee must distribute all the income. In a ***discretionary trust***, the trustee has discretion to distribute either the income or the principal or both.

1.   Trustee's Duty--

Marsman v. Nasca, 573 N.E.2d 1025 (Mass. 1991).

Facts. Testator was survived by her second husband (H), for whom she provided in a trust. Trustee (T) was directed to pay quarterly income to H and, after having considered H's sources of income, to pay principal for H's comfortable support and maintenance. H obtained title by operation of law to the Wellesley home owned as tenants by the entirety, but testator also indicated in her will her intent to convey the property to H. Upon Testator's death, Farr, the attorney, met with H. H was forced to reduce his style of living dramatically and to apply for a mortgage to pay bills. Farr was aware of H's status because he replied to an inquiry of the mortgage bank and H had asked Farr for money on one occasion. Farr asked H to support his need in writing and wrote to H that Farr thought the trust language was "broad enough to permit a distribution of principal." H never asked again from the date of Testator's death in 1971 until H was admitted to a nursing home in 1983. Farr had given him only $300 beyond the income of the trust. H remarried in 1972 and executed a simple will drafted by Farr, leaving most of H's property to his wife (P). By 1974, H could not meet expenses and conveyed his home to Testator's daughter by a former marriage and her husband. The daughter took over the mortgage payments, taxes, insurance, and major repairs. H retained a life estate. Farr had never advised H he could use the trust principal for the expenses of the home. The daughter died before H. Upon H's death the daughter's husband asked P to vacate. P brought this action in probate court. The court found T in breach of his duty to H and ordered the husband to convey the home to P and also ordered Farr to reimburse Testator's daughter's husband from the remaining portion of H's trust for the expenses he and Testator's daughter had paid for the upkeep of the property. If the trust was insufficient, the court found Farr personally liable. P appeals the denial of attorneys' fees. Testator's daughter's husband and Farr appeal from the denial of their motions to amend the findings and for a new trial.

Issues.

(i)   Does a trustee, holding a discretionary power to pay principal for the "comfortable support and maintenance" of a beneficiary, have a duty to inquire into the financial resources of that beneficiary so as to recognize his needs?

(ii)   If so, was the court's remedy for such failure correct?

Held. (i) Yes. (ii) No. Judgment vacated and remanded.

♦   The requirement that a trustee's power must be exercised with sound judgment following from a due appreciation of trust responsibility imposes upon a trustee a duty of inquiry into the beneficiary's needs.

♦   T also failed to meet his responsibilities of distribution under the trust.

♦   The conveyance was supported by sufficient consideration, and Testator's daughter and her husband had no notice of a breach of trust and were not themselves guilty of a breach of fiduciary duty; they cannot be charged as constructive trustees of the property.

♦ The remedy for T's failure to expend trust principal in this circumstance is to impress a constructive trust on the amounts that should have been distributed but were not because of T's error. On remand these amounts will be determined and paid to H's estate.

♦ The exculpatory clause in Testator's will, drafted by Farr and holding Farr harmless, was incorrectly invalidated by the probate court since there was no evidence that the insertion of the clause was an abuse of Farr's fiduciary relationship with Testator at the time the will was drawn.

♦ Farr's actions were not breaches of trust committed in bad faith or intentionally or with reckless indifference. Nor were they willful neglect.

D. RIGHTS OF THE BENEFICIARY'S CREDITORS

1. Creditors' Rights in Support Trusts and Discretionary Trusts.

a. Support trusts. A support trust is one in which the trustee is directed to make distributions as necessary for the education and maintenance of the beneficiary, and to expend the income and principal only for that purpose. In a support trust, creditors of the beneficiary cannot reach the beneficiary's interest. However, suppliers of necessaries may recover through the beneficiary's right to support.

b. Discretionary trusts. A discretionary trust is one in which the trustee is given discretion whether to apply or withhold payments of income or principal to or from a particular beneficiary, or (in some cases) to distribute the same to some other beneficiary. Before the trustee exercises her discretion to make payments to the beneficiary, the beneficiary's interest cannot be reached by his creditors. If, however, the trustee decides to pay over or to apply some amount of trust income or principal to the beneficiary, the right thereto vests in the beneficiary and his creditors may then reach it.

2. Spendthrift Trusts. In a spendthrift trust, the beneficiaries cannot voluntarily alienate their interests and their interests are protected from creditors.

a. Tort creditor--

Scheffel v. Krueger, 782 A.2d 410 (N.H. 2001).

Facts. Lorie Scheffel (P), individually and as the mother of Cory, filed suit against Krueger (D1), alleging that he had assaulted the minor, videotaped the assault, and broadcasted it over the Internet. (This conduct also formed the basis for criminal charges against D1.) Default judgment was entered against D1 and he was ordered to pay $551,286 in damages in the civil suit. P sought an attachment of an irrevocable trust in which D1 had a beneficial interest. The trust had been established by D1's grandmother for D1's benefit. The terms direct the trustee to pay the net income to D1 quarterly or more often if he so requests in writing. The trustee has the discretion to pay any principal to D1 for maintenance, support, and education. D1 may not invade the principal until he is 50 years of age, and he is prohibited from making any voluntary or involuntary transfers of his interest in the trust. The trustee's (D2) motion to dismiss P's claim was granted. P appeals.

Issue. Under the governing statute, RSA 564:23, does a trust's spendthrift provision bar claims brought by tort creditors?

Held. Yes. Judgment affirmed.

♦   The statute provides two exceptions to the enforceability of the spendthrift provision: where the beneficiary is the settlor and the trust is not a special needs trust and where the assets were fraudulently transferred to the trust.

♦   The statute clearly states that a creditor cannot subject the beneficiary's interest to the payment of its claim. There is no language to suggest a tort creditor should be exempt from the spendthrift provision.

♦   Where the legislature has provided exemptions, we cannot presume others were intended but not mentioned.

♦   P argues that the trust should be terminated because its purpose cannot be satisfied since D1 may be incarcerated for many years. However, the trust's purpose may still be fulfilled while D1 is incarcerated and after he is released.

Comment. RSA 564:23 was repealed in 2004.

---

   b.   **Alimony and child support--**

Shelley v. Shelley, 354 P.2d 282 (Or. 1960).

Facts. In his will, Grant Shelley's father left his residuary estate in trust for Grant. The income was to be paid to Grant for life, and the trustee was to start distributing the principal to Grant after he reached the age of 30. The trust contained a spendthrift clause, and the trustee had the discretion to distribute the principal to Grant or his children in case of an emergency requiring unusual expenditures. Grant married and divorced twice and had two children from each marriage. He was ordered to pay child support for all four children and alimony to his second wife. However, Grant disappeared, and the trustee bank (D) filed an interpleader in response to the claims under the divorce decrees.

Issue. Is a spendthrift provision of a trust effective against the claims of the beneficiary's former spouse for alimony and for support of the beneficiary's child?

Held. No. Decree affirmed in part and reversed in part.

♦ Although a trust is a spendthrift trust or trust for support, the interest of the beneficiary can be reached in satisfaction of an enforceable claim by the spouse or child of a beneficiary for child support, or by the spouse for alimony. The privilege of disposing of property is not absolute; it is hedged with various restrictions where there are policy considerations warranting the limitation.

♦ Public policy requires that the interest of the beneficiary of a trust should be subject to claims for child support. It is clear that parents have the obligation to support their children. Were we to bar claims for support, we would have the spectacle of a parent enjoying the benefits of a trust while the community pays for the support of the children. With regard to alimony for the spouse, the same considerations apply; in many cases, if the beneficiary's interest cannot be reached, the state may be called upon to support the spouse.

♦ We hold that the beneficiary's interest in the income of the trust is subject to the claims for alimony and to the claims for support of the children as provided under both divorce decrees. We adopt the view, however, that the claimants may reach only that much of the income that the trial court deems reasonable.

♦ The trust states that disbursements to Grant Shelley's children were to be made "in case of any emergency whereby unusual and extraordinary expenses are necessary. . . ." D claims that the expenses claimed in this case are not unusual or extraordinary. We disagree. We construe the clause to include the circumstances involved here—where the children are deserted by their father and are in need of support.

───────────

3. **Self-Settled Asset Protection Trusts.** It has long been recognized in trust law that one cannot protect himself from creditors by creating a trust for his own benefit. A result of this is the popularity of off-shore asset protection trusts. Some states have responded with a radical departure in American law. In 1997, Alaska and Delaware altered their trust statutes to legalize a spendthrift clause in a self-settled trust. These states also eliminated the rule against perpetuities. Without limiting the trust duration to the life of some person living at the time the trust is created plus 21 years, asset protection trusts can continue indefinitely in those states. In Missouri, there has been a limited exception to the rule that invalidates

self-settled spendthrift trusts since the 1980s. The exception does not apply where the trustor is the sole beneficiary of the income, the principal, or a fixed portion of either. Because the exception is so limited, however, Missouri is not as attractive as Alaska, Delaware, and sites outside the United States.

a. Off-shore trust--

Federal Trade Commission v. Affordable Media, LLC, 179 F.3d 1228 (9th Cir. 1999).

Facts. The Andersons (Ds), a married couple, formed Financial Growth Consultants, LLC, and sold the opportunity to participate in selling various products through late-night commercials. The Ponzi scheme (a scam in which subsequent investments are used to pay the promised yields to earlier investors) promised a 50% return in 60 to 90 days. Thousands of investors lost money, but Ds had tucked away their profits in a Cook Islands trust. They had created an irrevocable trust and were co-trustees with AsiaCiti Trust Limited, a company licensed to conduct trustee services under Cook Island law. The Federal Trade Commission (P) brought a civil suit against the Andersons to recover investors' profits, but the Andersons claimed they had relinquished all control over the assets of the trust. The court granted P's request for an ex parte temporary restraining order and later entered a preliminary injunction, which incorporated the provisions of the restraining order and required Ds to repatriate any assets held for their benefit outside of the United States. Ds faxed AsiaCiti and requested that the funds be repatriated so they could be held under the control of the court, but AsiaCiti replied that the court order was an event of duress under the terms of the trust, removed Ds as trustees, and refused to return their proceeds or provide an accounting. After P moved to find Ds in contempt, the court delayed ruling several times to allow Ds to purge themselves of their contempt. During the delays, Ds tried to appoint their children as trustees, but AsiaCiti removed them from acting as trustees because the event of duress was continuing. At a hearing, the court indicated that it did not believe that Ds had no control over the trust, and Ds were then found in contempt and placed in custody. Ds appeal.

Issue. Is it impossible to comply with a court order to repatriate assets held in an offshore asset protection trust if the defendant is a protector of the trust?

Held. No. Judgment affirmed.

♦ A party's inability to comply with a court order is a defense to a charge of civil contempt. Ds' inability, however, is a deliberate and intended result of their own actions. They created the trust to protect their assets from business risks and liabilities. Their inability and the trustee's refusal are the very goals of Ds' trust.

♦ Such "asset protection trusts" are designed to shield wealth by moving assets from the control of United States courts' jurisdictions.

♦ We are not satisfied that Ds have shown that it is impossible for them to comply with the court's order. We share the district court's skepticism that rational people would send millions of dollars outside of the country and retain absolutely no control over the money. Indeed, Ds obtained over $1 million from the trust to pay taxes.

♦ Ds' trust gives them affirmative powers to appoint new trustees and subjects the anti-duress provision to the protector's powers. It is significant that, after P revealed Ds' role as protectors of the trust, Ds immediately tried to resign as protectors. This indicates that Ds knew that, as protectors of the trust, they remained in control and could force the trustee to repatriate the assets.

Comment. The trust protector is created by the trust instrument in order to provide flexibility and to serve as a check on the trustees.

---

4. **Medicaid Trusts.** To qualify for Medicaid, an individual's financial resources must not exceed a few thousand dollars. Whether trusts that provide support to the individual are counted among the individual's resources for Medicaid purposes depends on the type of trust.

 a. **Discretionary trusts.** If an individual's assets form all or part of the trust and if the trust was established by the individual, a spouse, or a person acting on the individual's behalf, for purposes of Medicaid, a trust is deemed to be created by the individual. All of the assets of a revocable trust are considered available resources. Any income or principal that may be paid to the individual under any circumstances under the terms of an irrevocable trust are considered resources.

 1) **Exceptions.** A discretionary trust created by will by one spouse for the benefit of the survivor is not deemed an available resource. If a trust is created for a disabled person to provide care for the individual over and above what Medicaid may provide, and there is a provision for the trust to reimburse Medicaid upon the individual's death, the trust is not considered an available resource.

 b. **Third-person trusts.** Income or principal actually or legally available to a beneficiary of a mandatory or support trust established by a third person is considered a resource. A discretionary trust giving the applicant no legal right to the income is not considered a resource available to the individual unless the purpose was to provide for the applicant's support.

 c. **Careful drafting.** This area of the law demands great caution. Judicial interpretations of trust language are not consistent. Public policy considerations are unsettled. What works in one jurisdiction may not work in another.

E. MODIFICATION AND TERMINATION OF TRUSTS

1. **Modification of Distributive Provisions.** Some courts will permit a deviation of the terms of an express gift in instances where an unforeseen emergency threatens the accomplishment of the testator's purpose.

   a. **Trust modification denied--**

In re **Trust of Stuchell,** 801 P.2d 852 (Or. 1990).

Facts. Petitioner's (P's) four children were remainder beneficiaries of a trust. One of them, Harrell, was mentally retarded and unable to live without assistance. Harrell lived in a state facility and received Medicaid and Social Security benefits, both of which have income and resource limitations for participants. P requested the court to approve a modification of the trust so as to prevent Harrell's remainder from being distributed to him if he survives the trust's income beneficiaries. The proposed modification was designed to prevent Harrell's disqualification for public assistance. P appeals from the trial court's dismissal of her petition.

Issue. Should P's proposed modification be approved?

Held. No. Judgment affirmed.

◆ P relies on common law authority for allowing a court to approve the proposed modification. A trust may be terminated under very limited circumstances: (i) all beneficiaries agree, (ii) no beneficiary is under a legal disability, and (iii) the trust's purposes would not be frustrated in doing so.

◆ To extend the rule, P relies on Restatement (Second) Trusts, section 167(1), which provides that a court may permit the trustee to do acts not authorized by the terms of the trust.

◆ However, Comment b to section 167(1) states that a court will not permit a deviation from the terms of a trust "merely because such deviation would be more advantageous to the beneficiaries than a compliance with such direction." This limitation precludes permitting the proposed amendment, the only purpose of which is to make the trust more advantageous to the beneficiaries.

---

2. **Termination of Trusts.** If the settlor and all beneficiaries consent, a trust may be terminated. The weight of authority provides, however, that a trust cannot be terminated prior to the time fixed for termination, even though all the beneficiaries consent, if termination would be contrary to a material purpose of the settlor.

a. Remaining material purpose--

In re Estate of Brown, 528 A.2d 752 (Vt. 1987).

Facts. Andrew Brown died in 1977, settling his entire estate in a trust. The relevant portion of the trust instrument provided that the trust would be used for the education of the children of his nephew, Woolson Brown. After this purpose was accomplished, the income from the trust and as much of the principal as was necessary would be used by the trustee for the care, maintenance, and welfare of Woolson Brown and his wife (Ps), so that they might live in the style and manner to which they were accustomed during the remainder of their natural lives. Upon their demise, any remainder of the trust was to be paid to their then-living children in equal shares.

The trustee complied with the terms of the trust by using the proceeds to pay for the education of the children of Ps. After he determined that their education was complete, the trustee began distribution of trust income to the lifetime beneficiaries, Ps.

In 1983, Ps petitioned the probate court for termination of trust, arguing that the sole remaining purpose of the trust was to maintain their lifestyle and that distribution of the remaining assets was necessary to accomplish this purpose. The remaindermen (Ps' children) filed consents to the proposed termination. The probate court denied the petition to terminate, and Ps appealed to the Washington Superior Court. The superior court reversed, concluding that continuation of the trust was no longer necessary because the only material purpose, the education of the children, had been accomplished. An appeal by the trustee followed.

Issue. If any material purpose of the trust remains to be accomplished, may the trust be terminated if all beneficiaries consent?

Held. No. Judgment reversed.

- ◆   An active trust may not be terminated, even with the consent of all the beneficiaries, if a material purpose of the settlor remains to be accomplished.

- ◆   If either a support trust or a spendthrift trust were involved, termination could not be compelled by the beneficiaries because a material purpose of the settlor would remain unsatisfied.

- ◆   The trust at issue does not qualify as a support trust. A support trust is created when the trustee is directed to use trust income or principal for the benefit of an individual, but only to the extent necessary to support the individual. Because the trustee must, at the very least, pay all of the trust income to Ps, the trust cannot be characterized as a support trust.

- ◆   The trust also does not qualify as a spendthrift trust. A trust in which by the terms of the trust or by statute a valid restraint on the voluntary and involuntary transfer of the interest of the beneficiary is imposed is a spendthrift trust. The terms of the trust instrument do not manifest Andrew Brown's intention to create a spendthrift trust. The mere fact that an interest in a trust is not transferable does not make the trust a spendthrift trust.

♦ Termination cannot be compelled here because a material purpose of the settlor remains unaccomplished. The settlor's intention to assure a lifelong income to Ps would be defeated if termination of the trust were allowed.

---

b. **Trusts remaining indestructible beyond the perpetuities period.** A trust is not void merely because it can extend beyond the perpetuities period. The Rule Against Perpetuities applies to interests in a trust and requires that they vest or fail within the period provided by the Rule, but it does not limit the duration of the trust. Nonetheless, a trust cannot remain indestructible by the beneficiaries beyond the perpetuities period.

IX. BUILDING FLEXIBILITY INTO TRUSTS: POWERS OF APPOINTMENT

A. INTRODUCTION

1. **Types of Powers.** The creator of a power of appointment is called the ***donor***. The person granted the power is called the ***donee***. Those persons to whom the donee may appoint property are the ***objects***.

   a. **General and special powers.** All powers of appointment can be divided into general powers and special powers. A general power is one exercisable in favor of the donee, her estate, her creditors, or the creditors of her estate. A special power is one not exercisable in favor of the donee, her estate, her creditors, or the creditors of her estate.

2. **Does the Appointive Property Belong to the Donor or the Donee?** Under the relation-back doctrine, the donee was considered to have authority to fill in blanks in the donor's will; property subject to a power of appointment was viewed as owned by the donor and the power was conceived as merely authority of the donee to do an act for the donor. Special powers are still treated according to this doctrine.

3. **Creditor's Right to Property Subject to a Power of Appointment--**

Irwin Union Bank & Trust Co. v. Long, 312 N.E.2d 908 (Ind. 1974).

Facts. In 1957, Victoria Long (D) obtained a judgment in the amount of $15,000 against Philip Long as part of a divorce decree. In this action, D seeks satisfaction of that judgment by pursuing funds allegedly owed to Philip as a result of a trust set up by Laura Long, his mother. D alleged that the Irwin Union Bank and Trust Company was indebted to Philip as the result of its position as trustee of the trust created by Laura. The trial court ordered that any income, property, or profits that were owed to Philip and not exempt from execution should be applied to the divorce judgment. Thereafter, the trial court ordered that 4% of the trust corpus that benefited Philip was not exempt from execution and could be levied upon by D. The primary issue raised on appeal is whether the trial court erred in allowing execution on the 4% of the trust corpus.

Issue. Can a creditor reach property covered by an unexercised power of appointment?

Held. No. Judgment of trial court reversed and case remanded.

♦ Where a beneficiary was given a power under a testamentary trust to distribute property not his own by electing to withdraw not more than 4% of the trust corpus under certain circumstances, the power given to the beneficiary was a "power of appointment," and the beneficiary's former wife was not entitled as a creditor under a divorce decree to reach property covered by a power of appointment that was unexercised.

♦ The beneficiary of a trust had no control over the trust corpus until he exercised his power of appointment and gave notice to the trustee that he wished to receive his 4% of the trust corpus. Until such exercise was made, the trustee had the absolute control and benefit of the trust corpus within the terms of the trust instrument.

---

4. **Tax Reasons for Creating Powers.** The donee of a general power of appointment over income or principal is regarded as the owner of that property. The income is taxable to the donee. If the power of appointment is exercised during the donee's lifetime, the transferred property is subject to gift taxation. If the power of appointment is not exercised during the donee's lifetime, the property is a part of the donee's federal gross estate and is subject to taxation. Note that property subject to a special power of appointment is not treated as owned by the donee.

B. CREATION OF A POWER OF APPOINTMENT

1. **Intent to Create a Power.** The creation of a power of appointment must be accompanied by the donor's express or implied manifestation of intent.

2. **Powers to Consume.** The issue of whether a power to consume principal has been created arises in connection with powers of appointment.

   a. **Inconsistent clauses in will--**

Sterner v. Nelson, 314 N.W.2d 263 (Neb. 1982).

Facts. The will of the decedent, Oscar Wurtele (T), bequeathed to his wife, Mary, all his property "absolutely with full power in her to make such disposition of said property as she may desire." It also provided that upon the death of his wife (or if she predeceased T), the remaining property should vest in T's foster daughter and her children (Ps). After T's death, Mary remarried. Mary died testate, leaving property to various individuals, including her husband, but not to Ps referred to in T's will. The trial court held that the language in T's will created a fee simple absolute in Mary. Ps appeal.

Issue. If a will conveys absolute title in fee simple, will an inconsistent clause in the instrument attempting merely to limit that title or convey to the same person a limited title be disregarded?

Held. Yes. Judgment affirmed.

♦ The general rule is that when there is a bequest to one in general terms only, expressing neither fee nor life estate, and there is a subsequent limitation over of what remains at the first taker's death, if there is also given to the first taker an unlimited and unrestricted power of absolute disposal, the bequest is construed to pass a fee. The attempted limitation over is void. If a will conveys an absolute title in fee simple, an inconsistent clause in the instrument attempting to limit that title or convey to the same person a limited title will be disregarded.

♦ Here, the grant to Mary Wurtele was clear and unambiguous. She was to have the property "absolutely with full power in her to make such disposition of said property as she may desire." We find no reason why the common law rule should not be applied to this bequest. Accordingly, we hold that the bequest to Mary Wurtele was a fee simple absolute.

---

b. **Taxation of powers to consume.** A power to consume that allows the donee to appoint property to himself during his lifetime is a general power of appointment and is taxable. However, if the power is limited by ascertainable standards, it falls within an exception and is not taxable.

C. RELEASE OF A POWER OF APPOINTMENT

Powers of appointment (except powers in trust or imperative powers) may be released in all jurisdictions, pursuant to case law or statute.

1. **Contract to Exercise a Power of Appointment--**

Seidel v. Werner, 364 N.Y.S.2d 963 (1975).

Facts. The decedent, Steven Werner, entered into a separation agreement with his second wife, Harriet, whereby he agreed to make a will in which he would exercise his testamentary power of appointment over his share of a trust, known as the Abraham Werner Trust No. 1, by establishing a trust for the benefit of their children, Anna and Frank Werner. Less than four months after the divorce judgment, of which the separation agreement was made a part, the decedent executed a will, which, instead of executing his testamentary power of appointment in favor of Anna and Frank Werner, left everything to his third wife, Edith (D). The trustees of the trust (Ps) are suing for a declaratory judgment to determine who is entitled to the decedent's share of the trust fund.

Issue. May the donee of a power of appointment that is not presently exercisable contract to make an appointment?

Held. No. Summary judgment granted for D.

♦   The donee of a power of appointment that is not presently exercisable, or of a postponed power that has not become exercisable, cannot contract to make an appointment. Such a contract cannot be the basis of an action for specific performance or damages, but the promisee can obtain restitution of the value given by him for the promise unless the donee has exercised the power pursuant to the contract.

♦   However, Harriet, Anna, and Frank Werner argue that at a minimum the agreement should be construed as a release of his power of appointment, and that Anna and Frank should be permitted to take as on default of appointment. This argument is inapplicable to this case since it is clear that the parties did not intend a release of the power of appointment. Nor is the effect of the promised exercise of the power the same as would follow from release of the power, since the agreement provides for appointment of a greater principal to Anna and Frank than they would get in default of appointment. Also, under the trust instrument, on default of exercise of the power, the property goes to the four children absolutely, whereas under the separation agreement, the decedent shall create a trust payable to Harriet as trustee for the support of Anna and Frank. Finally, under the separation agreement, if Anna and Frank fail to qualify, the principal would go to the decedent's estate, whereas under the trust instrument, in default of appointment and an inability of Anna and Frank to take, the decedent's share would go to his other children, if living, and if not, to his next of kin. Under these circumstances, it is too strained to construe the separation agreement as the equivalent of a release of the power of appointment. Accordingly, D is entitled to the decedent's share in the principal of the Abraham Werner trust.

D.   EXERCISE OF A POWER OF APPOINTMENT

1.   **Exercise by Residuary Clause in Donee's Will.** Courts are split over whether a residuary clause should presumptively exercise a general or special power of appointment. The Uniform Probate Code, section 2-610, provides that a general residuary clause in a will, or a will making general disposition of all of the testator's property, does not exercise a power of appointment held by the testator unless specific reference is made to the power or there is some other indication of intention to include the property subject to the power.

a.   **Partial release of general power of appointment--**

Beals v. State Street Bank & Trust Co., 326 N.E.2d 896 (Mass. 1975).

Facts. The will of the decedent, Arthur Hunnewell (T), placed the residue of his property in a trust, the income of which was to be paid to his wife during her life. The will directed that at the death of the wife the trust was to be divided into portions, one for each surviving daughter and for the then-surviving issue of any deceased daughter. The will directed that the income of each portion should be, on a daughter's death, paid and disposed of as she may direct and appoint by her last will. Following the death of her mother, one daughter, Isabella Hunnewell Dexter, requested the trustees to make the principal payments by transferring virtually all of her trust share to the Dexter family office in Boston. Thereafter, Isabella executed an instrument partially releasing her general power of appointment under her father's will. Isabella, who died without issue, did not expressly exercise her power of appointment under her father's will but did leave a will that left the residue of her estate to the issue of her sister Margaret Blake, who had predeceased Isabella. In default of appointment, the Blake issue would take one-half of Isabella's trust share. If Isabella's will should be treated as effectively exercising her power of appointment, the Blake issue would take the entire trust share and the executors of the will of Isabella's sister Jane would not receive that one-half of the trust share that would otherwise go to Jane in default of appointment. The trustees (Ps) of T's will filed a petition for instructions, seeking a determination of the distribution to be made. The trial court reserved decision and reported the case to the appeals court. The case was then transferred to the supreme court.

Issue. Does the partial release of a general power of appointment obviate the application of the rule of construction that presumes that a general residuary clause exercises a general power of appointment?

Held. No. Judgment so ordered.

- ♦ We are unaware of any decided case that, in this context, has dealt with a testamentary general power reduced to a special power by action of the donee. We conclude that the residuary clause of Isabella's will should be presumed to have exercised the power of appointment. We believe that a presumption of exercise is more appropriate in this case than a presumption of nonexercise.

- ♦ When this court first decided not to extend to a special power of appointment the rule of construction that a general residuary clause executes a general testamentary power unless a contrary intent is shown by the will, we noted significant distinctions between a general power and a special power. A general power was said to be a close approximation of a property interest while a special power lacked this quality.

- ♦ The rationale for the canon of construction applicable to general powers should be applied in this case. The power was a general power at its inception. Isabella had the use and enjoyment of the major portions of the property and this is a factor properly considered as weighing in favor of the exercise of a power of appointment by a will. Here, the partial release of a general power does not obviate the application of that rule of construction that presumes that a general residuary clause exercises a general power of appointment.

---

2. **Limitations on Exercise of a Special Power.** Donees of general powers of appointment can usually appoint outright or in further trust. They can also create new powers of appointment. The donee's authority is more limited with a special power of appointment. A special power must be exercised in accordance with the instrument creating the power, and the donor may impose restrictions on the way the power may be exercised.

   a. **Creation of limited interest.** Unless the donor has expressed a contrary intent, the donee of a special power may appoint limited interests to objects of the power, or appoint in further trust. In some states the donee of a special power may not appoint in further trust unless it appears that the donor intended to allow such an appointment. The rationale for this minority view is that the donor presumptively intended that the trust be terminated and the assets distributed to persons selected by the donee. The special power gives the donee only the right to select the recipients.

   b. **Exclusive and nonexclusive powers.** A special power is either exclusive or nonexclusive. If the donor intends that the donee be able to exclude one or more of the class of objects, perhaps appointing all the property to one object, the power is exclusive. If the donor intends that all members of the class benefit, but that the amount of each share shall be determined by the donee, the power is nonexclusive. The presumption is that the donor intends the power to be exclusive. However, courts often have found that the presumption is overcome by particular language in the creating instrument.

3. **Fraud on a Special Power.** The donee of a special power may not appoint to non-objects of the power. If the donee of a special power appoints to a class composed of objects and non-objects, the appointment to the non-objects is void. An appointment to an object with an express condition that the object pay over an amount to a non-object is a fraudulent appointment. The condition is void. If the donee of a special power appoints to an object in consideration of a benefit to a non-object, the appointment is void to the extent it was motivated by the purpose of benefiting non-objects.

4. **Ineffective Exercise of the Power.** If an attempted exercise of a power of appointment is ineffective, the donee's intent may still be effectuated by allocation and capture.

   a. **Allocation of assets.** Under the doctrine of allocation, when the donee of a power blends her own property with the appointive property, and exercises the power in an invalid way, the donee's own property and the appointive property will be allocated, if possible, to give maximum effect to the donee's intent. Thus, the donee's own property may be allocated to the appointees, and the appointive property may be allocated to legatees of the donee's own property.

b. **Capture.** Ordinarily, if the donee of a power makes an ineffective exercise, the property goes in default of appointment. If there is no gift in default, the property reverts to the donor or the donor's estate. The exception to this is the capture doctrine. If the donee of a general power of appointment ineffectively exercises the power, but manifests an intent to assume control of the appointive property for all purposes, the property is captured in the donee's estate. The question is whether the donee intended to capture the property; if so, the property does not pass in default of appointment. The intent to capture the property can be found in a general blending clause in a will that expresses the donee's intent to dispose of her own property and any property over which she has power of appointment. An intent to capture can also be found in a residuary clause that disposes of the donee's property and the appointive assets in the same manner.

E. FAILURE TO EXERCISE A POWER OF APPOINTMENT

Appointive property passes in default of appointment if the donee of a general power fails to exercise it. The property reverts to the donor's estate if there is no gift in default of appointment. Appointive property passes to the objects of the power if they are an ascertainable, limited class if the donee of a special power fails to exercise it and there is no gift in default of appointment.

1. **Disposition of Property When Special Power of Appointment Is Not Exercised--**

Loring v. Marshall, 484 N.E.2d 1315 (Mass. 1985).

Facts. Marian Hovey (T) died in 1898, survived by a brother, a sister, and two nephews. By her will, T left the residue of her estate in trust, the income payable in equal shares to her brother and sister during their lives. Upon her brother's death in 1900, his share of the income passed to her sister, and, upon her sister's death in 1922, the income was paid in equal shares to her two nephews. One nephew died in 1928, unmarried and without issue. His share of the income then passed to his brother who remained the sole income beneficiary until his death in 1946.

T's will gave Cabot Jackson Morse, the surviving nephew, a special power to appoint the trust principal to his "wife and issue" with the limitation that only income could be appointed to a widow who was living at T's death. Cabot was survived by his wife Anna, who was living at T's death, and by his only child, Cabot Jr., who died in 1948, two years after his father. Cabot left a will, which provided that the power of appointment he had under T's will was to be exercised by appointing to his wife the right to the income during her lifetime. Consequently, the trust income following Cabot's death was paid to Anna until her death in 1983, when the principal became distributable. The trustees thereupon sought instructions as to who is entitled to the remainder of the Marian Hovey Trust now that the trust is distributable. Among the claimants are several charities who were to receive the whole trust fund if neither nephew left appointees.

Issue. If the donee of a special power of appointment fails to exercise it and there is no gift in default of appointment, may the appointive property pass to the objects of the power?

Held. Yes. Judgment so ordered.

- ♦ When a special power of appointment is not exercised, and absent specific language indicating an express gift in default of appointment, the property not appointed goes in equal shares to the members of the class to whom the property could have been appointed.

- ♦ Applying this rule of law, there is no specific language in the will indicating a gift in default of appointment in the event Cabot should fail to appoint the principal.

- ♦ T's will discloses an intent to keep her property in the family. The interests T gave to her sister and brother were life interests, as were the interests given to her nephews. The share of any nephew who died unmarried and without issue, as one did, was added to the share of the other nephew. Each nephew was limited to exercising his power of appointment in favor of his issue and his widow. The apparent intent to keep the assets within the family is sufficiently strong to overcome any claim that T's will provides for a gift to the charities in default of appointment.

- ♦ The testamentary trust provided that the last surviving income beneficiary had a power of appointment of trust principal, but the last surviving income beneficiary of the trust appointed only the trust income. In the absence of any express gift in default of appointment, the surviving issue of the donee of the power of appointment (*i.e.,* the estate of Cabot Jr.) was entitled to distribution of the trust principal.

————————

X. CONSTRUCTION OF TRUSTS: FUTURE INTERESTS

A. INTRODUCTION

A future interest is a nonpossessory interest capable of becoming possessory in the future. The law of future interests deals with situations where the beneficial enjoyment of land by a successor occurs at some time in the future. Certainty of beneficial enjoyment is not required; however, there must be at least the possibility of future beneficial enjoyment.

B. CLASSIFICATION OF FUTURE INTERESTS

1. **Future Interests in the Transferor.** The three types of future interests that can be retained by the transferor are *reversion, possibility of reverter*, and *right of entry*. These interests will or may become possessory in the transferor or her successors in interest.

    a. **Reversion.** A reversion is a future interest left in the grantor after she conveys a vested estate of a lesser quantum than she has (usually a life estate).

    b. **Possibility of reverter.** A possibility of reverter arises when a grantor carves out of her estate a determinable estate of the same quantum (the determinable estate will end if some future event occurs).

    c. **Right of entry.** A right of entry occurs when a grantor creates an estate subject to a condition subsequent and retains the power to cut short or terminate the estate upon the happening of that condition.

2. **Future Interests in Transferees.** The three types of future interests in transferees are *vested remainders*, *contingent remainders*, and *executory interests*.

    a. **Remainders.** A remainder is a future interest created in a grantee that is capable of becoming a present possessory estate upon the expiration of a prior possessory estate created in the same conveyance in which the remainder is created. A *vested* remainder is created in an ascertained person in being and is not subject to a condition precedent (*i.e.*, it is capable of becoming possessory whenever the preceding estate terminates). A *contingent* remainder, on the other hand, is created in an unascertained person or is subject to a condition precedent (*i.e.,* it is contingent on something happening before it can become possessory).

    b. **Executory interests.** Any interest in a transferee that cannot be a remainder must be an executory interest. An executory interest is a future interest that must, in order to become possessory, divest or cut short some interest in another transferee (a shifting executory interest) or divest the transferor following a certain period of time during which no transferee is entitled to possession (a springing executory interest).

3. **Destructibility of Contingent Remainders.** This doctrine holds that if a legal contingent remainder in land does not vest before or at the termination of the preceding freehold estate, the remainder is destroyed. In about three-fourths of the states, the destructibility rule has been abolished by statute or judicial decision.

C. CONSTRUCTION OF TRUST INSTRUMENTS

1. **Preference for Vested Interests.** If an interest might be classified as vested or contingent, the common law preference is to classify it as vested.

   a. **Transferability and taxation.** Over 40 states have made contingent interests transferable by statute or judicial decision. Reversions, remainders, and executory interests are descendible and devisable at death in the same manner as possessory interests. The federal government subjects to gift or estate taxation any gratuitous transfer of a property interest.

   b. **Acceleration into possession.**

      1) **Renunciation valid--**

In re **Estate of Gilbert,** 592 N.Y.S.2d 224 (1992).

Facts. Lester Gilbert (D) renounced his share of two wholly discretionary trusts under his father's will. The estate was worth $40 million. D, age 32, had no children and was a member of a group of people who shared a similar religious doctrine. The executor (P) petitions this court to declare D's renunciation null and void.

Issues.

(i) Would permitting the renunciation violate the testator's intent to provide for D?

(ii) Does D possess a current property interest that he can renounce?

Held. (i) No. (ii) Yes. Judgment for D.

♦ The decedent's intention is not controlling. The law does not compel a man to accept an estate against his will.

♦ The controlling statutes provide that a beneficiary of a disposition may renounce all or part of his interest in a transfer of property by a person during his lifetime or by will. Property is "anything that may be the subject of ownership."

- D's renunciation applies to his remainder interest in one elective share trust, contingent upon D surviving his mother, and to his current interest in a trust under which he may have the right to compel the trustees to distribute trust property to him under certain circumstances.

- The filing of a renunciation has the same effect with respect to the renounced interest as if D had predeceased his father without issue.

___

    c.   **Requiring survival to time of possession.** Generally, a remainderman need not live to the time of possession. If the remainderman predeceases the life tenant, the remainder passes to his estate. The testator may, however, expressly require survival, and in some cases courts will infer a requirement of survival.

        1)   **Present vested interest--**

First National Bank of Bar Harbor v. Anthony, 557 A.2d 957 (Me. 1989).

Facts. Franklin Anthony (T) created a revocable inter vivos trust providing for income to be paid to him for life, then to his widow, should she survive him, and upon her death the corpus was to be divided in equal shares to T's three children: John, Peter, and Dencie. T's wife and John predeceased T. Upon T's death, his will was admitted to probate and left two-thirds of T's estate to Peter and one-third to Dencie; John's children (Ds) were expressly omitted. Ds filed a motion for summary judgment, asserting John's interest in the trust was vested, not contingent, at the time of its creation. The summary judgment motion was granted against Ds. Ds appeal.

Issue. Was John's remainder interest a present, vested interest at the time of the creation of the inter vivos trust?

Held. Yes. Judgment vacated.

- Because a will is not operative until the testator's death, an interest in a testamentary trust cannot vest prior to the death. An inter vivos trust is operative from the date of creation.

- The terms of T's trust included T's right to change beneficiaries, an absence of control over how the children might dispose of their shares, and no condition of survival of any children. This plan effectively eliminated any further interest of T unless he chose to intervene.

- T's failure to change the trust terms suggests a disposition to a predeceased child's estate rather than a reversion.

Comment. Other states have held that an inter vivos trust reserving to the settlor income for life plus power to revoke, with a remainder over at the settlor's death, creates a vested interest in the remaindermen subject to defeasance by exercise of the revocation power. Enjoyment is postponed until termination of the life estates, but upon execution of the trust instrument, there is a present right to the remainder.

---

2) Common law rule where bequest is to be paid at certain age--

---

Clobberie's Case, 86 Eng. Rep. 476 (1677).

Facts. A sum of money was bequeathed to a woman to be paid to her with interest upon her reaching the age of 21 or upon the day of her marriage. She died before either condition was satisfied.

Issue. If a bequest is to be paid on the express condition that the beneficiary reach a certain age, and that condition does not occur, does the bequest pass to the estate of the beneficiary?

Held. Yes.

♦   When a sum of money is to be paid to a woman upon her reaching the age of 21 or upon her day of marriage, and she dies before either condition is met, the bequest passes to her executor as part of her estate. However, if the money were bequeathed to one "at" the age of 21, then the bequest would lapse.

---

3) **Controversial change in UPC section 2-707.** A few states (Alaska, Colorado, Hawaii, Michigan, Montana, and New Mexico) have adopted a highly controversial 1990 change made by the revisers of the UPC to section 2-707. Under the new language, absent language to the contrary, the following rules apply:

   (i)   All future interests in trust are contingent on the beneficiary's surviving to the date of distribution.

   (ii) If a remainderman does not survive to the distribution date, UPC section 2-707 creates a substitute gift in the remainderman's descendents who survive the date of distribution.

   (iii) If a remainderman dies before distribution and leaves no descendents, the remainder fails, and, if there is no alternative remainder that takes effect, the trust property passes to the settlor's residuary devisees or the settlor's heirs.

This provision destroys the flexibility of the common law and the transmissible remainder rule; the beneficiary may no longer devise the remainder to whomever he pleases. Spouses suffer most, as only issue are substituted for the deceased remaindermen. The change presents numerous problems for estate planners; to insulate their trusts from the problems inherent in section 2-707, planners in states where the section has been adopted can include in their trust instruments a general disclaimer that totally disclaims the rules of construction embodied in section 2-707.

2. Gifts to Classes.

a. Gifts of income.

1) Construing class gift to testator's grandchildren--

Dewire v. Haveles, 534 N.E.2d 782 (Mass. 1989).

Facts. A petition for a declaration of rights was brought seeking construction of a will creating a class gift on behalf of Thomas Dewire's (T's) grandchildren. T died in January 1941 survived by his widow, his son (Thomas Jr.), and three grandchildren. His will placed substantially all of his estate in a residuary trust. The trust income was payable to his widow for life and on her death to Thomas Jr. and Thomas Jr.'s widow and children. After T's death, Thomas Jr. had three more children by a second wife. Thomas Jr. died in 1978, a widower, survived by all six of his children. Thomas III, who had served as trustee since 1978, died in 1987 leaving a widow and one child, Jennifer. The question presented is whether Jennifer takes her deceased father's share in the trust income or whether the remaining class members (the other five grandchildren) take that income share equally by right of survivorship.

In his will, T provided that his grandchildren share equally in the net income of his estate. There is no explicit provision in the will concerning the distribution of income on the death of a grandchild, nor is there any statement as to what the trustee should do with trust income between the death of the last grandchild and the date assigned for termination of the trust 21 years after that event.

Issue. Is the daughter of T's deceased grandchild entitled to succeed by right of representation to the grandchild's income interest in a trust created by a class gift?

Held. Yes. Judgment so ordered.

♦   The gift of net income to T's grandchildren, divided equally or to be shared equally, is a class gift. The class includes all six grandchildren, three of whom were born before and three of whom were born after T's death.

- In the absence of a contrary intent expressed in the will or a controlling statute stating otherwise, members of a class are joint tenants with rights of survivorship.

- T's will violated the Rule Against Perpetuities because Thomas Jr. could (and did) have children after T's death; the trust was thus scheduled to terminate 21 years after a life not necessarily yet in being. Nevertheless, the language of this void provision can be used to determine T's intention as to dispositions that do not violate the Rule.

- T provided that the trust should terminate 21 years after the death of his last grandchild. It is unlikely that T intended that trust income should be accumulated for 21 years. He must have expected that someone would receive the income during those years. The only logical recipients would be the issue (by right of representation) of deceased grandchildren, the same group of people who would take the trust assets on termination of the trust (assuming no violation of the Rule Against Perpetuities).

- Since every other provision in the will concerning the distribution of trust income and principal (after the death of T and his wife) points to equal treatment of T's issue per stirpes, there is a sufficient contrary intent shown to overcome the rule of construction that the class gift of income to grandchildren is given to them as joint tenants with the right of survivorship. Thus, Jennifer in her lifetime is entitled to one-sixth of the net income of the trust during the period of the class gift of income.

---

b. **Gifts to children or issue.**

1) **Meaning of "children" and "issue."** The word "children" does not include grandchildren. The word "issue" includes grandchildren and more remote descendants.

2) **UPC section 2-705.** Adopted persons and persons born out of wedlock are included in class gift terminology in accordance with rules for determining relationships for purposes of intestate succession. However, a person born out of wedlock is not treated as the child of the father unless he is openly and notoriously so treated by the father.

c. **Gifts to heirs.**

1) **Determining identity of heirs--**

Estate of Woodworth, 22 Cal. Rptr. 2d 676 (1993).

Facts. Harold Woodworth's (T's) testamentary trust established by T's will provided for a portion of T's estate to go to T's wife (W) as life tenant and to terminate upon W's death. The remaining trust estate was to go to T's daughter (D) if she survived and if not, then to D's heirs at law. Upon D's death in 1980, she was survived by her husband (H), a niece, and a nephew. H died testate in 1988, leaving the residue of his estate to the Regents of the University of California (Rs) for the university's Berkeley campus. W died in 1991. The trustee bank (P) petitioned the probate court to determine D's heirs at law. The court determined the niece and nephew to be D's heirs. Rs appeal.

Issue. Absent evidence of T's intent to the contrary, must the identity of "heirs" entitled to trust assets be determined at the date of the death of the named ancestor who predeceased the life tenant, and not at the date of the death of the life tenant?

Held. Yes. Judgment reversed.

♦ There is a common law preference for vested rather than contingent remainders, unless an instrument discloses a different intent. Thus, a remainder to a class became vested in the class when one or more of its members came into existence and could be ascertained, even though the class is subject to open.

♦ When a gift is made to "heirs," the donor is saying he wants the property distributed as if the named person died intestate. Thus, the death of the named individual is the normal time for applying the statute of descent or distribution, absent a manifested intent by T that the statute be applied earlier or later.

♦ None of the exceptions to the early vesting rule reflected in *Wells Fargo Bank v. Title Insurance & Trust Co.,* 22 Cal. App. 3d 295, 99 Cal. Rptr. 464 (1971), applies here. This is not a situation where the "life tenant is the sole heir, but the will devises the remainder to the testator's heirs."

♦ We have nothing before us that reveals T's intent and nothing forecloses the possibility that T took into account that D might predecease and H might outlive W.

♦ There is no language in the decree that contains any expression of futurity in the description of the ancestor's heirs, such as "my then living heirs at law." The word "then" here merely indicates time of enjoyment.

---

2) **The doctrine of worthier title.** The doctrine of worthier title provides that if a settlor transfers property in trust but retains a life estate in himself or another, and attempts to create a remainder in his heirs, a presumption arises that the settlor intended to retain a reversion in himself instead of a remainder in his heirs. The doctrine is a rule of construction, not a rule of law. It raises a presumption that no remainder in the settlor's heirs has been created, but this presumption

can be rebutted by evidence of a contrary intent of the grantor. The doctrine may still exist in some states.

3) **The rule in *Shelley's Case*.** The rule in *Shelley's Case* states that if one instrument creates a freehold in land in A and purports to create a remainder in A's heirs and the estates are both legal or both equitable, then the remainder becomes a remainder in fee simple in A. It is a legal principle that applies notwithstanding the transferor's intent. The rule has been abolished in nearly all states.

d. **The rule of convenience.** Under the rule of convenience, a class closes when any member has the right to demand distribution of her share, and not when the beneficiary actually demands distribution or when distribution occurs. If no members of the class have been born before the testator's death, the class does not close until the death of the designated ancestor of the class. If there is an immediate bequest of a separate fixed sum to each member of a class, the class closes at the testator's death, even if there are no members of the class alive. If the gift is postponed in possession after a life estate, the class will not close under the rule of convenience until the time for taking possession.

1) **Class closes when all existing members reach stated age--**

Lux v. Lux, 288 A.2d 701 (R.I. 1972).

Facts. The will of the decedent, Philomena Lux (T), provided that in the event that her husband, Anthony Lux, predeceased her, the residue of her estate should go to her grandchildren, share and share alike. It further provided that any real estate included in the residue shall be maintained for the benefit of the grandchildren and shall not be sold until the youngest of the grandchildren has reached 21 years of age. T was survived by one son (Anthony) and five grandchildren. The youngest grandchild was born after the execution of the will but before T's death. The son informed the trial court that he and his wife plan to have more children. The trial court appointed a guardian ad litem to represent the interests of the grandchildren. It also appointed an attorney to represent the rights of individuals who are unknown but who may have an interest under the will.

Issue. When all existent members of a class have attained the stated age, should the class be closed and the distribution be made?

Held. Yes. Judgment so ordered.

♦ We hold that the distribution of the trust corpus shall be made at any time when the youngest of the then-living grandchildren has attained the age of 21. When all existent members of the class have attained the stated age, considerations of convenience require that distribution shall then be made and that the property shall not be kept from further utilization to await the uncertain conception of further members of the group.

♦ Should it become necessary due to a decline in rental income to sell the property, the trustee has the discretionary power to sell the real estate. The proceeds from the sale shall, because of the doctrine of the substitute res, replace the realty as the trust corpus. Income would be payable to the beneficiaries as it accrues. Should additional children be born, the amount of each share of income received by a grandchild would be reduced as each new member of the class joins his brothers and sisters.

XI. TRUST DURATION AND THE RULE AGAINST PERPETUITIES

A. INTRODUCTION

1. **Development of the Rule.** The Rule Against Perpetuities states: "No interest is good unless it must vest, if at all, not later than 21 years after some life in being at the creation of the interest." [John C. Gray, The Rule Against Perpetuities, §201 (4th Ed. 1942)] An early formulation of the Rule was announced in the *Duke of Norfolk's Case* in 1682, and the Rule was further refined over the next few centuries as courts sought to prevent long-term restrictions on the alienability of land.

2. **Policies Underlying the Rule.** The Rule is designed to further marketability of property and prevent an undue concentration of wealth in the hands of the few. The Rule also encourages the socially desirable result that wealth be controlled by the living and not by the dead. It also curtails trusts, which can protect wealthy beneficiaries from bankruptcies and creditors.

3. **When the Lives in Being Are Ascertained.** The validity of an interest is determined as of the time of the purported creation of the interest. "Lives in being" must be persons alive at that time. Generally, the perpetuities period (lives in being plus 21 years) begins to run whenever the transferor makes an irrevocable transfer. If the interest is created by will, the period begins at the testator's death. If the interest is created by deed, or by an irrevocable deed of trust, the period begins at the time the deed is delivered with intent to pass title. If a trust is revocable by the settlor, the period begins at the date the trust becomes irrevocable.

4. **The Validating Life.** For an interest to be valid, the necessary proof must be made from among persons who can affect vesting. Alternatively, the interest must vest at creation, or vest or fail within 21 years after creation.

B. THE REQUIREMENT OF NO POSSIBILITY OF REMOTE VESTING

Under the common law rule, any possibility of remote vesting voids the interest. About half the states have reformed this what-might-happen rule. One of the reforms is the wait-and-see doctrine (covered below).

1. **The "Fertile Octogenarian."** The law conclusively presumes that a person can have children as long as the person is alive. A few states have enacted legislation to deal with the conclusive presumption of fertility, prescribing that

any person who has attained the age of 65 shall be deemed incapable of having a child.

2. **The "Unborn Widow."** The law presumes that a person's surviving spouse might turn out to be a person not now alive.

   a. **Example.** O devises "to A for life, then to A's wife for life, then to A's children who survive A's widow." It is possible that A may marry someone not in being (not yet born) at O's death (which is the time of the transfer). She could live beyond lives in being (O's life and A's life) plus 21 years. Therefore, the devise to the children is void. This is the case of the "unborn widow."

   b. **Bare possibility is sufficient--**

Dickerson v. Union National Bank of Little Rock, 595 S.W.2d 677 (Ark. 1980).

Facts. Nina Dickerson (T) was survived by her two children. Cecil (P), 50, was single, and Martin, 45, was married. At that time the two sons had a total of seven children, who were T's grandchildren. T named the bank (D) as executor and directed that at the close of administration proceedings D transfer to itself as trustee all the assets of the estate. The will required the trust to continue until the death of both sons and Martin's widow, and the youngest child of either son has reached the age of 25. At that time, the trust was to distribute and pay over the entire balance of the trust fund to the bodily heirs of both of her sons.

T died in 1967. The probate court entered a routine order reciting that the will had been properly executed and approving the executor's first and final accounting and closing the administration of the estate. The order makes no reference to the validity of the trust or the manner in which the assets of the estate were to be distributed.

In 1977, P filed a complaint against D and its trust officer. The complaint asserted that the trust was void under the Rule Against Perpetuities. The complaint charges the trust officer with violations of his fiduciary duties in failing to deliver all the estate assets to T's heirs and in failing to ask the probate court to construe the will with respect to violations of the Rule Against Perpetuities. The chancery court rejected P's attack on two grounds. First, P should have raised the question of the validity of the trust in the probate court in connection with the probate of the will and the administration of the estate. His failure to do so makes the issue res judicata. Second, on the merits, the trust does not violate the Rule Against Perpetuities.

Issue. Is a trust created by a will void under the Rule Against Perpetuities because it is possible that the interest of the various beneficiaries might not vest within the period allowed by that rule?

Held. Yes. Chancery court judgment reversed and case remanded.

♦ Failure of a will beneficiary to challenge the validity of a trust as violative of the Rule Against Perpetuities in probate proceedings does not preclude him from raising that issue in a later action, where the validity of the trust was not necessarily within the issues before the probate court and the probate court made no pertinent decisions as to the validity of the trust.

♦ Since the bank was both executor of the estate and trustee of the trust established in the will, the bank was a fiduciary and owed a duty of good faith and loyalty to all beneficiaries of the estate and of the trust. Therefore, the bank could not ignore the possible invalidity of the trust both in probate court and in ex parte chancery court proceedings and then take advantage, to its own pecuniary benefit, of the beneficiaries' similar course of conduct by asserting that the beneficiaries' failure to challenge the validity of the trust in probate proceedings precluded P from raising that issue in a later action.

♦ A bare possibility that a beneficiary's interest will not vest within the period allowed by the Rule Against Perpetuities is enough to render that interest void.

♦ The terms of this trust present an instance of the "unborn widow." This trust is not to terminate until the deaths of P, Martin, and Martin's widow, but the identity of Martin's widow cannot be known until his death. Martin might marry an 18-year-old woman 20 years after his mother's death, have additional children by her, and then die. P might also die. Martin's young widow, however, might live for another 40 or 50 years, after which the interests would finally vest. But since P and Martin would have been the last measuring lives in being at T's death, the trust property would not vest until many years past the maximum time allowed by the Rule. The trust is therefore void because there is a possibility that the estate will not vest within a period measured by a life or lives in being at T's death, plus 21 years.

---

    c.   **Split contingencies.** If the transferor makes a gift upon either of two contingencies, one of which must occur within the perpetuities period, and the other of which might not, the contingencies are judged separately. The gift is valid if the first contingency occurs; the second contingency is void.

C. APPLICATION OF THE RULE TO CLASS GIFTS

    1.   **The Basic Rule: All or Nothing.** Pursuant to the Rule, a class gift must be valid as to all members of the class or it is completely void. It cannot be valid as to some members and invalid as to others. If the gift to one member of the class might vest too remotely to satisfy the Rule, the entire class gift is void. The *rule of convenience* may operate to save some class gifts.

a. **Consequences of violating the rule.** Violation of the Rule will result in the violating interest being stricken, with all other valid interests left standing.

2. **Gifts to Subclasses.** One exception to the all or nothing class gift rule is the doctrine of subclasses. Under this doctrine, a remainder held to be invalid as violative of the Rule Against Perpetuities does not taint and invalidate all other remainders where the ultimate takers are not described as a single class but as a group of subclasses.

    a. **Remainders to other subclasses not invalidated.** *American Security & Trust Co. v. Cramer*, 175 F. Supp. 367 (D.D.C. 1959), involved a devise of remainders to subclasses. Abraham Hazen bequeathed property in trust to his wife for life, then to his daughter for life, then to her children for their lives. Upon the death of each of Abraham's grandchildren, the decedent's share of the estate would "go absolutely to the persons who shall then be her or his heirs at law." Because the will made a gift to each grandchild instead of a gift to the next generation upon the death of all of the grandchildren, the court applied the "gifts to subclasses" exception to the class gift rule. The gifts over following the life estates in two grandchildren who were not alive when the testator died were void, leaving a reversion in Abraham's estate. However, the gifts over following the life estates in two grandchildren who were living when the testator died were valid and were not affected by the two invalid remainders because the four remainders were to subclasses and stood separately.

3. **Specific Sum to Each Class Member.** Another exception to the all or nothing class gift rule is where there is a gift of a stated sum to every member of the class. The policy underlying this exception is that the amount intended by the conveyor to be given to each class member can be deduced without estimating how many persons are in the class.

4. **Does Vest = Vest = Vest?** Difficulties arise regarding the meaning of the word vest, since orthodox doctrine has insisted that whether an interest is vested or contingent depends upon the form of words set forth in the limitation.

D. APPLICATION OF THE RULE TO POWERS OF APPOINTMENT

To apply the Rule Against Perpetuities to powers of appointment, the powers must be separated into (i) general powers presently exercisable, which are treated as absolute ownership for purposes of the Rule, and (ii) general testamentary powers and all special powers.

1. **General Powers Presently Exercisable.**

    a. **Validity of power.** A general inter vivos power is valid if there is certainty that the power will vest or fail within the perpetuities period. Once the power becomes exercisable, the property is no longer tied up. The fact that the donee may exercise the power after lives in being plus 21 years is irrelevant.

b. **Validity of interests created by exercise of a general power presently exercisable.** An interest created by exercise of a general power is deemed valid according to the same principles as if the donee owned the property in fee. The perpetuities period runs from the exercise of the power.

2. **General Testamentary Powers and Special Powers.**

   a. **Validity of power.** A testamentary or special power is valid if it may not be exercised beyond the perpetuities period that begins at the creation of the power. If the power may be exercised beyond the perpetuities period, it is void ab initio.

   b. **Validity of exercise.** General and special powers are treated alike when determining the validity of an appointment. The perpetuities period begins at the date the power was created.

      1) **The "Delaware tax trap."** Under Delaware law, every interest created by the exercise of all powers must vest within the perpetuities period. This provision theoretically would permit life estates to be created in indefinite succession through the exercise of successive special powers of appointment, thus avoiding federal tax liability (since property subject to a special power of appointment is not taxable at the donee's death). However, section 2041(a)(3) of the Internal Revenue Code taxes the assets in the donee's estate if he exercises his special power of appointment by establishing another power that can be exercised regardless of the first power's date of creation.

      2) **The second-look doctrine.** Under the second-look doctrine, the exercise of a power of appointment is read back into the instrument that created the power, and the facts existing on the date of the exercise of the power are taken into consideration. Thus, the court will determine if the interests vest or fail within the time prescribed by the rule, taking into account the facts existing on the date of the appointment.

   c. **Rule applied to partial power of revocation.** In *Second National Bank of New Haven v. Harris Trust & Savings Bank*, 283 A.2d 226 (Conn. 1971), the issue was whether the interests created in a will were valid under the Rule Against Perpetuities. In 1922, Caroline Trowbridge created an inter vivos trust that gave her daughter, Margaret, a life interest income and a testamentary power of appointment. Caroline reserved the power to revoke, modify, or alter the terms of the trust respecting payment of the income, but not the principal. In 1929, Margaret gave birth to

Mary. Caroline died in 1941, and Margaret died in 1969. Through her will, Margaret exercised the power of appointment by creating another trust that gave Mary income for 30 years and then the principal, if Mary was still living. If Mary died during the 30-year period, the principal was to go to Mary's issue per stirpes. The court determined that the perpetuities period began when the trust was created in 1922, rather than at the time of Caroline's death in 1941, because the trust was revocable only as to the income interest, and thus it was not equivalent to absolute ownership. Therefore, the court held that the Rule Against Perpetuities would not invalidate the gifts of the trust income and the principal to Mary because both of these gifts vested in interest at the death of Margaret, whose life was a measuring life, but the rule barred the contingent remainder to Mary's children or their descendants because it could have vested more than 21 years after Margaret's death.

E. SAVING CLAUSES

A saving clause rectifies any possible violation of the Rule. Such a clause should be included even in those jurisdictions that have adopted a cy pres or "wait-and-see" doctrine.

1. **Attorney Liability for Violating Rule.** Courts are divided as to whether an attorney who drafts a will that violates the Rule is liable for negligence.

F. PERPETUITIES REFORM

Three kinds of reform have emerged to alleviate some of the harsh effects of the Rule: the wait-and-see doctrine, the equitable reformation or cy pres doctrine, and remedying the most objectionable applications of the Rule with specific remedies.

1. **The "Wait-and-See Doctrine."** Under this doctrine, the validity of interests is judged by actual events as they happen, and not by events that might happen. [*See In re* Estate of Anderson, 541 So. 2d 423 (Miss. 1989)]

    a. **Statutory period applies to nonvested interest created pursuant to power of appointment--**

In re **Trust of Wold,** 708 A.2d 787 (N.J. 1998).

Facts. Seward Johnson (of Johnson & Johnson) created trusts in 1944 to benefit his children; Elaine Johnson Wold (P) is the beneficiary of the trusts. Under the terms of the trust, the trustees were directed to collect income, pay expenses payable out of income, and accumulate the net income until P reached the age of 21. At that time, the trustees had absolute discretion to pay to P as much of the income as the trustees deemed to be for her best interest. The trust also permits the trustees to transfer and pay to "the life beneficiary"

(P) "any or all of the trust property." Upon P's death, the trustees are directed to pay over the trust property to her spouse and issue as directed in her will or, in the absence of a will, to her issue in equal shares. P wishes to create a testamentary trust appointing the proceeds of her trust in further trust for the benefit of her spouse and surviving issue. The new trust would permit property held by one of P's children to continue in trust for that child's issue upon the child's death. Thus, the issue's (P's grandchild's) interest would be considered nonvested since the property would pass only upon the happening of a specific event, the death of P's child. P plans to rely on the New Jersey "wait and see" 90-year perpetuities period and has requested the trustees to petition this court for direction and interpretation regarding the application of the New Jersey statute to her proposed exercise of her power of appointment under the terms of the 1944 trust.

Issues.

(i) Does the power granted to P to dispose of the trust res include the power to appoint the trust assets by a successive testamentary trust?

(ii) Does the New Jersey Uniform Rule Against Perpetuities, which provides that an act that would have been invalid at common law is nevertheless valid if it vests within 90 years of its creation and becomes invalid only if it continues in existence and does not vest within that time period, apply to a nonvested interest created pursuant to the exercise of a power of appointment vested in P by a 1944 trust and measured from the creation of the 1944 trust?

Held. (i) Yes. (ii) Yes. Judgment for P.

♦ The trustees have been given the maximum flexibility and discretion in addressing the beneficiary's needs.

♦ The law of trusts supports P's position. The Restatement (Second) of Trusts, section 17, provides that a trust may be created by "a person having a power of appointment to another person as trustee for the donee of the power or for a third person."

♦ The settlor's clear purpose in establishing the trust was to protect the trust from tax burdens to the fullest extent of the law. The proposed testamentary trust will effect significant tax savings. Such a purpose, rather than being restricted, is well within the contemplation and intent of the trust instrument.

♦ While the New Jersey statute generally may not apply retroactively, where the applicability of a new statutory period is being determined, the law states that an interest created pursuant to a power of appointment is deemed created upon the exercise of that power. Thus, if the power created by P were exercised after July 3, 1991 (the effective date of the statute), the Rule would apply to an interest created under that power.

Comment. The New Jersey Uniform Statutory Rule Against Perpetuities was repealed in 1999. It was replaced with a statute that allows a perpetual trust if the trustee has either an expressed or implied power to sell or an unlimited power to terminate the trust in one or more living persons.

_____

2. **The Uniform Statutory Rule Against Perpetuities (1986, as amended in 1990).** The Uniform Statutory Rule Against Perpetuities ("USRAP") provides for two rules against perpetuities, the common law Rule and the wait-and-see rule of 90 years. The original drafters of USRAP failed to notice the effect of this provision when conjoined with the generation-skipping transfer tax (a tax payable on the transfer to a person who is at least two generations removed from the transferor). Pursuant to treasury regulations in effect when USRAP was enacted, the generation-skipping transfer tax does not apply to trusts created prior to 1986 unless the exercise of a special power of appointment delays the vesting of an interest beyond the common law perpetuities period. Under USRAP, a grandfathered trust is not exempt if a special power of appointment is exercised in violation of the common law perpetuities period, thus giving rise to the 90-year wait-and-see rule. In 1990, section 1(e) was added to USRAP, providing that if the vesting of a gift is based on two alternative contingencies, one of which complies with the common law perpetuities period and the other with the USRAP period, effect is given only to the common law perpetuities period.

3. **Cy Pres or Equitable Reformation.** Under this doctrine, an invalid interest is reformed within the limits of the Rule to approximate most closely the intention of the creator of the interest.

G. THE RULE AGAINST SUSPENSION OF THE POWER OF ALIENATION: NEW YORK LAW

1. **A Brief Explanation of the Suspension Rule.** The rule prohibiting suspension of the power of alienation proceeds upon a policy assumption that the power of alienation is suspended only when there are not persons in being who can convey an absolute fee. The rule applies only if the taker of a contingent interest is unborn or unascertainable. Subsequent modifications of the statute have made it similar in scope to the common law Rule Against Perpetuities, with the exception that trusts that might last beyond the statutory period are more likely to be held invalid under the statute than they would be under the Rule.

2. **Application of the Suspension Rule to Statutory Spendthrift Trusts.** The power of alienation is suspended when a transfer is made in trust if (i) the legal fee simple to the trust property is nontransferable or (ii) the equitable owners cannot convey possessory interests in absolute fee.

XII. CHARITABLE TRUSTS

A. NATURE OF CHARITABLE PURPOSES

A charitable trust is one for the benefit of a class of persons, and not for the benefit of the community at large, and must be for relief of poverty or for the advancement of education, religion, health, or other charitable purpose. It must benefit the general public or some particular class of the public that is indefinite in number.

1. Creation of a Charitable Trust--

Shenandoah Valley National Bank v. Taylor, 63 S.E.2d 786 (Va. 1951).

Facts. The will of the decedent, Charles Henry, provided that the residue of his estate was to be held in trust by the Shenandoah Valley National Bank of Winchester, to be paid by the trustee on the last school days of each calendar year before Christmas and Easter "in as many equal parts as there are children in the first, second, and third grades of the John Kerr School of the City of Winchester, and (the trustee) shall pay one of each such equal parts to each child in such grades, to be used by such child in the furtherance of his or her obtainment of an education." One of the next of kin of the decedent (P) filed suit against the executor and trustee (Ds) challenging the validity of the will, which undertook to create a charitable trust. P argued that the trust did not constitute a charitable trust and was invalid in that it violated the Rule Against Perpetuities. The trial court held that the trust was not charitable but was a private trust, and thus violated the Rule Against Perpetuities and was void.

Issue. Must a trust be public in nature before it will be considered a charitable trust?

Held. Yes. Decrees affirmed.

♦   A charitable trust is created only if the settlor properly manifests an intention to create a charitable trust. Charitable purposes include the relief of poverty and the advancement of education, religion, health, municipal purposes, and other purposes the accomplishment of which are beneficial to the community. It is essential that the charity be for the benefit of an indefinite number of persons, for if all the beneficiaries are personally designated, the trust lacks the essential element of indefiniteness, which is one characteristic of a legal charity.

♦   Here, the time for payment of the funds to the children is when their minds would be far removed from studies and indicates that no educational purpose was in the testator's mind. Execution of the mandate of the trust accomplishes no educational purpose. It merely places the income forever beyond the range of the trust. The words of the trust import an intent to have the trustee pay each child an allotted share. The testator's intent was to bestow upon each child gifts that would bring happiness on the two holidays, which purpose falls far short of an educational trust.

♦   It is argued that even if the will fails to create a charitable trust for educational purposes, it nonetheless produces a desirable social effect. We disagree. A trust from which the income is to be paid at stated intervals to each member of a designated segment of the public, without regard to whether the recipients are poor or in need, is not for the relief of poverty, nor is it a social benefit to the community. There is no language in this will that permits the trustee to limit the recipients to the schoolchildren who are in necessitous circumstances. Accordingly, it is mere benevolence—a private trust—and not a charitable trust.

_____

B. MODIFICATION OF CHARITABLE TRUSTS: CY PRES

Where a general charitable bequest is impracticable, some courts will execute a gift cy pres through a scheme framed by the court for the purpose of carrying out the general purpose.

1. General Charitable Purpose--

In re **Neher,** 18 N.E.2d 625 (N.Y. 1939).

Facts. Ella Neher's (T's) will devised certain real property to the village (P), with a direction that P erect a hospital named as a memorial to T's deceased husband. P accepted the property in 1931. In 1937, P petitioned the surrogate's court to construe and reform the relevant provision of T's will, directing that P would receive the property and erect an administration building in T's husband's memory since a nearby hospital adequately served P's needs. P's petition was denied. The appellate division affirmed. P appeals.

Issue. Was T's devise a general intention to devote the property to charitable purposes instead of a specific intention to limit the use of the property to the operation of a hospital?

Held. Yes. Order reversed and remanded.

♦   This was a gift to the entire community. That was the first stated design of beneficence.

♦   The direction that a hospital be erected shows an absence of particularity as to type, management, or control, except that P's trustees were to be the governing board. This absence of particularity is a strong showing against the view that the instruction was the substance of the gift.

♦   We think T's intention was a general charitable gift with an added graft as to T's desires. A graft may be ignored when compliance is altogether impracticable, and the gift may be executed cy pres through a scheme devised by the court to carry out the general charitable purpose.

---

2. Great Increase in Available Funds--

In re **Estate of Buck,** 21 U.S.F. L. Rev. 691 (Cal. Sup. Ct. 1987).

Facts. In 1975, Beryl Buck (T) died a resident of Marin County, California. Marin County is the most affluent county in the San Francisco Bay Area and is the nation's second-wealthiest county of more than 50,000 residents. T's will left the residue of her estate to the San Francisco Foundation, a community trust administering charitable funds in five counties in the Bay Area. Her will directed that the residue of her estate be used for exclusively nonprofit charitable, religious, or educational purposes in providing care for the needy in Marin County, and for other nonprofit charitable, religious, or educational purposes in that county.

At the time of T's death, the largest asset in her estate consisted of a block of stock worth about $9 million. In 1979, Shell Oil won a bidding war and bought the stock in the Buck Trust for $260 million, which increased to well over $300 million by 1984. In 1984, the foundation brought suit seeking judicial authorization to spend some portion of the Buck Trust income in the other four counties of the Bay Area. The foundation's petition for cy pres rested upon the following theory: The enormous increase in the value of principal was a change in circumstances raising substantial doubt whether T, had she anticipated such an event, would have limited her beneficence to Marin County. Forty-six individuals and charitable organizations in the other four counties (called "objector-beneficiaries") were allowed to intervene to object to the Marin-only limitation.

Issue. Does the doctrine of cy pres apply if there is a dramatic, unexpected increase in trust funds and a different use of trust funds would be more advantageous to the community?

Held. No. Judgment denied the petition for modification.

♦   Cy pres applies only where the purpose of a trust has become illegal, impossible, or permanently impracticable of performance, and the testator manifested a general charitable intention. In practice, cy pres has most often been applied in California in such cases where the charitable trust purpose is literally impossible to fulfill or in cases where it has become reasonably impossible of performance. Ineffective philanthropy, inefficiency, and relative inefficiency (*i.e.*, inefficiency of trust expenditures in one location given greater relative needs or benefits elsewhere) do not constitute impracticability.

♦   If both the testator's intent and the charitable gift can, in fact, be effectuated, *i.e.*, the specified trust purpose has not become impossible or impracticable of performance, there is no justification for cy pres. Cy pres may not be invoked upon the belief that the modified scheme would be more desirable or would constitute a better use of the income. Courts have held that terms of a charitable trust may not be modified on the grounds that a different use would be more beneficial to the community or advantageous to the charity. Cy pres does not authorize the court to vary the terms of a trust merely because the variation will meet the desire and suit the convenience of the trustee.

C. SUPERVISION OF CHARITABLE TRUSTS

Most states authorize their attorney general to enforce charitable trusts on behalf of a community. Others with a particular identifiable interest in the trust may also enforce the trust.

1. **Donor Has No Standing.** In *Carl J. Herzog Foundation, Inc. v. University of Bridgeport*, 699 A.2d 995 (Conn. 1997), the court considered a donor's standing under the Uniform Management of Institutional Funds Act ("UMIFA"). In 1986, the Herzog Foundation made a gift to the University of Bridgeport for nursing scholarships. In 1991, the nursing school closed, and the funds were added to the university's general endowment. The foundation brought suit for an injunction to reestablish the scholarships or to give the money to a foundation that would administer the nursing scholarships. The court held that the donor of a charitable gift does not have standing to enforce the terms of a gift unless he expressly reserved that right. Generally, such gifts are enforceable by the attorney general. The foundation argued that it had standing under UMIFA, which supplements cy pres with a provision releasing an institution from a donative restriction with the donor's written consent or, if the donor is dead, disabled, or otherwise unavailable, with court approval. However, the court held that "[t]he drafters of UMIFA expressly provided that the donor of a completed gift would not have standing to enforce the terms of the gift."

2. **Donor Has Standing--**

Smithers v. St. Luke's-Roosevelt Hospital Center, 723 N.Y.S.2d 426 (2001).

Facts. Smithers, decedent and recovered alcoholic, made a gift of $10 million over time to St. Luke's Roosevelt Hospital Center (D) to set up an alcoholism treatment center. In his letter to D creating the gift, Smithers stated that project plans and staffing had to have his approval. D agreed to use the gift to expand its alcoholism treatment practices to include rehabilitation in a free-standing environment removed from the hospital setting. D purchased the free-standing building with $1 million of the first installment of the gift and opened its Smithers Alcoholism Treatment and Training Center. Smithers continued to be involved in the management of the Center in an uneasy relationship with D. In

1978, Smithers wrote D that it had not lived up to his letter of intent, and no more money would be forthcoming. In 1981, D's president, Gambuti, began discussions with Smithers to induce him to continue the gift. Smithers was repeatedly assured that D would strictly adhere to the terms of the gift. Smithers agreed to complete the gift and did so in 1983 with a letter stating that the final installment would be set aside in an endowment fund, and the income was to be used only for the support of the Center. Any unused money remaining at the end of the calendar year was to be accumulated and added to the principal. The principal was to be used only for repairing and remodeling the Center building or any other building space used directly in conjunction with the Center. Gambuti acknowledged in writing the acceptance of the gift subject to the restrictions. From 1992 until his death in 1994, Smithers joined Gambuti in successfully soliciting millions of dollars in donations for a total restoration of the Center building. One year after Smithers died, D announced its plans to sell the building and move the Center into a hospital ward. Mrs. Smithers (P) notified D of her objections and demanded an accounting of the Center's finances. D disclosed that it had been misappropriating money from the endowment fund since before Smithers's death. It had used the money for unrelated hospital purposes. After P notified the attorney general, D returned almost $5 million to the endowment fund. Subsequently, P and the attorney general tried for three years to negotiate a resolution with D, but were unsuccessful. However, in 1998, D entered into an agreement with the attorney general to make no more transfers or loans from gift funds and to return to the fund $1 million from the sale of the building. P, who had been appointed special administratrix of Smithers's estate for the purpose of pursuing the estate's claims, brought suit against D and the attorney general to enforce the conditions of the gift and to obtain an accounting. D moved to dismiss for lack of standing, and the attorney general moved to dismiss for lack of standing and for failure to state a cause of action. The motions were granted. P appeals.

Issue. Does the estate of the donor of a charitable gift have standing to sue the donee to enforce the terms of the gift?

Held. Yes. Complaint reinstated.

♦ The attorney general's office (under the direction of a newly elected attorney general) maintains that only the attorney general has standing to enforce the terms of the gift at issue here and that the proposed settlement between the attorney general and D has resolved all of the issues. While the attorney general, by statute, represents the beneficiaries of charitable dispositions, the attorney general's standing in these actions is not exclusive.

♦ The rule barring beneficiaries from suing charitable organizations is not applicable here. P did not bring this action on behalf of the beneficiaries of the Center or on her own behalf. She brought this action as the court-appointed special administratrix of her late husband's estate to enforce his rights under the agreement with D through specific performance.

♦ The donor of a charitable gift is in a better position than the attorney general to be vigilant and to enforce his own intent, which is entitled to protection.

♦ This case shows the need for coexistent standing for donors and the attorney general. Their distinct but related interests are best served if donors have standing to enforce the terms of their gifts along with the attorney general's standing to enforce gifts on behalf of the beneficiaries.

Dissent. When a charitable gift is made without provision for a reversion to the donor or his heirs, their interests are permanently excluded.

XIII. TRUST ADMINISTRATION: THE FIDUCIARY OBLIGATION

A. INTRODUCTION

By creating a trust, a settlor interposes a trustee between the beneficiary and the property, thereby relieving the beneficiary from the burdens associated with property management. However, a trustee does not have a direct financial incentive to act with loyalty and care in managing the trust fund. It is the beneficiary, rather than the trustee, who bears the risk and receives the rewards of the trustee's good or bad management. To safeguard the beneficiary against a trustee's mismanagement or misappropriation, the trustee is held to a fiduciary standard of conduct. The fiduciary obligation comprises the duties of loyalty and prudence and rules that reinforce these duties.

B. THE DUTY OF LOYALTY

1. **No Self-Dealing.** A trustee has a duty to give undivided loyalty to the beneficiaries. The duty of loyalty requires trustees to avoid any conflicts of interest between personal interests and the interests of the trust or estate. Thus, ***any*** transactions between the individual and the trust or estate should be avoided. A trustee who engages in self-dealing is liable even if he acted in good faith and treated the beneficiaries fairly. The trustee's only defense to self-dealing is consent by the beneficiaries after full disclosure (the transaction must still be fair and reasonable).

   a. **Trustee's wife acts as purchaser--**

Hartman v. Hartle, 122 A. 615 (N.J. 1923).

Facts. The testator, Dorothea Geick (T), named her two sons-in-law executors and directed them to sell her real estate and divide the proceeds equally among her five children. The executors sold part of the real estate to one of T's sons, who bought the property for his sister, the wife of one of the executors. She sold the property two months later for a $1,600 profit. One of T's daughters (P) filed a bill charging the sale to have been improper and fraudulent.

Issue. Is the sale of property by an executor to his wife, without previous authority from the court, illegal and void?

Held. Yes. Decree will be advised.

♦   The settled law in this state is that a trustee cannot purchase from himself at his own sale, and his wife is subject to the same disability.

- Because the property is now owned by innocent purchasers, the executors and the wife will be held accountable for P's one-fifth share of the profits on resale.

---

b. Conflict of interest--

In re **Rothko,** 372 N.E.2d 291 (N.Y. 1977).

Facts. The decedent, Mark Rothko (T), an internationally known painter, died testate, leaving an estate consisting principally of 798 paintings. Bernard Reis, Theodoros Stamos, and Morton Levine were appointed co-executors (Ds). Within three weeks of their appointment, Ds agreed to sell to Marlborough A.G., a Liechtenstein corporation, 100 paintings to be paid for in interest-free installments over a 12-year period after an initial payment of $200,000. They also consigned to Marlborough Gallery, Inc., a domestic corporation, some 700 other paintings listed in a schedule to be prepared. It later came to light that Reis was a director, secretary, and treasurer of Marlborough Gallery in addition to being co-executor of the estate; that Stamos was a not-too-successful artist financially and that it was to his advantage to curry favor with Marlborough Gallery; and that Levine failed to exercise ordinary prudence because he was aware of Reis's conflict of interest. Kate Rothko, T's daughter, later joined by her brother, Christopher Rothko, and the attorney general of the state (Ps), brought suit to remove Ds, to enjoin the sale of the paintings, to rescind the agreements entered into, to have returned the paintings still in possession of the corporations, and for damages. The trial court held for Ps. The appellate court affirmed. This appeal followed, Ds contending that they acted in good faith and that the plan was fair.

Issue. While a trustee is administering a trust, must he refrain from placing himself in a position where his personal interest may conflict with the interest of the beneficiaries?

Held. Yes. Order affirmed.

- The duty of loyalty imposed on a fiduciary prevents him from accepting employment from a third party who is entering into a business transaction with the trust. While the fiduciary as trustee is administering the trust, he must refrain from placing himself in a position where his personal interest or that of a third person does or may conflict with the interest of the beneficiaries. Here, to assert that there was no conflict of interest on the part of Reis and Stamos is to indulge in sheer fantasy. Reis was not only a director and officer of Marlborough Gallery but had financial inducements to favor Marlborough through sales of his own extensive art collection. So too did Stamos benefit as an artist under contract with Marlborough.

- Levine argues that, having acted prudently and upon the advice of counsel, a complete defense is established. We disagree. An executor who knows that his co-executor is committing breaches of trust and who not only fails to exert efforts directed toward prevention but accedes to the breaches is legally accountable even though he was acting on the advice of counsel.

♦ We now turn to the proper measure of damages. In general, when a trustee is authorized to sell trust property, but in breach of trust sells it for less than he should receive, he is liable for the value of the property at the time of the sale less the amount that he received. If the breach of trust consists only in selling it for too little, the trustee is not chargeable with the amount of any subsequent increase in value of the property. However, if the breach consists of some misfeasance other than solely selling for too low a price, appreciation damages may be appropriate. A trustee may be held liable for appreciation damages if it was his duty to retain the property. The same rule should apply here where there is a serious conflict of interest.

---

c. **Co-trustees.** A co-trustee does not have the power to transfer or deal with the property without consulting the other co-trustees. Nor may a trustee delegate decisionmaking powers to a co-trustee. These powers can only be exercised by the co-trustees together.

d. **Insider trading.** Under Securities Exchange Commission Rule 10b-5, a person with inside information about a stock cannot buy or sell the stock unless he first discloses this information. A fiduciary will be bound by this rule since the obligations of a fiduciary do not include the performing of an illegal act.

C. THE DUTY OF PRUDENCE

Under the Uniform Prudent Investor Act, a trustee must observe the standards in dealing with the trust assets that would be observed by a prudent person dealing with the property of another. If the trustee has special skills or is named trustee on the basis of representations of special skills or expertise, he is under a duty to use those skills. The trustee must consider the following factors before investing: (i) safety of principal, (ii) liquidity, and (iii) rate of return.

1. Duty to Diversify--

Estate of Collins, 139 Cal. Rptr. 644 (1977).

Facts. The will of the decedent, Ralph Collins, authorized the trustees (Ds), the decedent's business partner and lawyer, to purchase every kind of property and make every kind of investment, and further provided that all discretion conferred upon the trustees shall be absolute. After the will was admitted to probate and distribution of the estate made, there was $50,000 remaining for Ds to invest. They loaned the money to two real estate developers, Downing and Ward, who assured Ds that they were not in default on any of their loans. Thereafter, Downing and Ward Construction Company went bankrupt, resulting in a loss to the trust fund of $60,000. Ds filed a petition for approval and for settling of the first and final account and for their discharge. The beneficiaries under the trust (Ps) objected on the basis that Ds had improperly invested the $50,000. The trial court held for Ds. Ps appeal.

Issue. Is a trustee under a duty to the beneficiaries to distribute the risk of loss by a reasonable diversification of investments?

Held. Yes. Judgment reversed.

♦ A trustee is under a duty to distribute the risk of loss by reasonable diversification. Here, Ds invested two-thirds of the trust principal in a single investment.

♦ The general rule is that second or other junior mortgages are not proper trust investments. Here, Ds invested in real property secured only by a second deed of trust.

♦ Also, in buying a mortgage for trust investments, the trustee should give careful attention to the valuation of the property, in order to make certain that the margin of security is adequate. Here, Ds invested without adequate investigation of either the borrowers or the collateral.

———————

2. **Balancing Gains and Losses.** Courts typically apply the prudent person standard to each investment decision of the trustee rather than to the trust portfolio as a whole. Thus, the trustee is not permitted to balance gains and losses if the breaches of trust are separate and distinct.

3. **ERISA.** The Employment Retirement Income Security Act of 1974 ("ERISA") provides rules governing investment of pension funds by the trustees managing the funds and imposes a prudent investor rule. The trustee must discharge his duties solely in the interest of the beneficiaries.

4. **Prudent Person Rule of Investment--**

In re **Estate of Janes**, 681 N.E.2d 332 (N.Y. 1997).

Facts. Janes's (T) estate, valued at $3.5 million, contained a stock portfolio valued at $2.5 million; 71% of that value came from 13,232 shares of Kodak. T bequeathed his estate to three trusts: a marital deduction trust for his wife, a charitable trust, and a trust providing income to his wife and a remainder to charity. The Lincoln Rochester Trust Company and Mrs. Janes acted as co-executors, and Lincoln First Bank (P) (the Rochester

Trust Company's successor) acted as trustee. After P's trust officers, Patterson and Young, determined estate assets and the administrative expenses of the estate, Patterson recommended, in August 1973, selling 800 shares of Kodak to cover the expenses. No investment strategies were discussed. One month later, at a meeting with Patterson and Young, Mrs. Janes consented to the sale of 1,200 additional shares of Kodak. She was told that P was retaining the rest of the Kodak shares, but the factors that would lead to an informed investment decision were not discussed. Mrs. Janes, 72, had a high school education, no business experience, and had never been employed. The value of the stock at the time was about $139 per share, making the estate's shares worth almost $1,840,000. By the end of 1973, the price of Kodak stock began to fall. By the time P filed its initial accounting in 1980, the share price was $47 per share and the shares held by the estate were worth $530,000. In 1981, P sought judicial settlement of its account. Mrs. Janes and later, the attorney general, on behalf of the charitable beneficiaries (collectively, "objectants"), filed objections, asserting that P's conduct violated the "prudent person rule" of investment. Upon Mrs. Janes's death in 1986, the personal representative of her estate was substituted for her as an objectant. At trial, after the court found that P had acted imprudently, the court used the "lost profits" or "market index" measure of damages, imposed more than a $6 million surcharge against P, and ordered P to forfeit its commissions and attorney's fees. The decision was upheld on appeal, but the damages were recalculated according to the "value of the capital that was lost" and were lowered to about $4 million. P and the objectants appeal.

Issue. Under the prudent person rule of investment, may a fiduciary be surcharged for imprudent management of a trust based upon a failure to diversify?

Held. Yes. Judgment affirmed.

♦   The prudent person rule of investment, followed by New York at the time of P's administration of the estate, provides that "[a] fiduciary holding funds for investment may invest the same in such securities as would be acquired by prudent [persons] of discretion and intelligence in such matters who are seeking reasonable income and the preservation of their capital."

♦   There is no precise formula for determining whether the prudent person standard for investment has been violated in a certain situation. Instead, an examination of the facts and circumstances of each case is required. The lack of specificity of the rule allows for the propriety of the trustee's investment decisions to be "measured in light of the business and economic circumstances existing at the time they were made."

♦   The factors to be considered include: the amount of the trust estate, the beneficiaries' situation, the trend of prices and the cost of living, the prospect of inflation and deflation, investment marketability, and potential tax consequences. Another factor affecting a particular investment decision, particularly relevant to this case, is the wisdom of the decision in light of the nature and objective of the trust, rather than merely the integrity of the particular investment.

- By retaining such a high concentration of Kodak stock, P paid insufficient attention to the needs of T's widow, the primary income beneficiary of the estate, and led to the eventual need to substantially invade the principal of the marital trust. A prudent investor would have sold the Kodak stock by August 1973. P's internal documents show that, by that time, P had all of the information a prudent investor needed to conclude that the estate was too heavily invested in the stock.

- The proper measure of damages for P's negligent retention of the concentration of Kodak stock in the estate's stock portfolio is the value of the capital that was lost, without considering lost profits or market index. Where a fiduciary's misjudgment consists solely of negligent retention of assets that should have been sold, the measure of damages is the value of the lost capital, as calculated by determining the value of the stock on the date it should have been sold, and subtracting from that figure the proceeds from the sale of stock or, if the stock is still held by the estate, the value of the stock at the time of the accounting.

---

5. **Duty Not to Delegate.** A trustee has a duty not to delegate acts that the trustee can reasonably be required to perform personally. He may delegate certain nondiscretionary functions, but he has a duty to supervise those to whom he delegates.

   a. **Delegation of investment power.** In *Shriners Hospitals for Crippled Children v. Gardiner*, 733 P.2d 1110 (Ariz. 1987), Laurabel Gardiner had established a trust to provide income to her daughter, Mary Jane, and her grandchildren, Charles and Robert. The remainder was to pass to Shriners Hospitals. Mary Jane was appointed trustee, Charles was named first alternate trustee, and Robert was second alternate trustee. Mary Jane, not an experienced investor, left all of the investment decisions to Charles, an investment counselor and stockbroker. Subsequently, Charles embezzled over $300,000 from the trust. Shriners brought a petition to surcharge Mary Jane for the full amount. The court found that Mary Jane breached her fiduciary duty by delegating her investment authority to Charles without retaining any control over investment decisions. A trustee is subject to liability for such conduct. However, the court explained that the loss was caused by Charles's diversion of funds, not by poor investment decisions. Therefore, unless Mary Jane's delegation of authority to Charles was the proximate cause of the loss, she would not be personally liable. The case was remanded for findings of fact on the question of causation.

6. **Liability for Contracts and Torts.** The traditional rule is that a trustee is personally liable on any contract the trustee makes, in the absence of express provision in the contract limiting the trustee's liability. A trustee is similarly liable in tort. A trustee is personally liable to the same extent that a beneficial owner of the trust property would be liable.

D. IMPARTIALITY AND THE PRINCIPAL AND INCOME PROBLEM

A trustee has a duty of impartiality between the income beneficiary and the remainderman, *i.e.*, she must act to produce a reasonable income while at the same time preserving the trust property for the remainderman.

1. Trustee's Duty of Impartiality--

Dennis v. Rhode Island Hospital Trust Co., 744 F.2d 893 (1st Cir. 1984).

Facts. The great-grandchildren of Alice Sullivan (Ps) are remaindermen of a trust established by their great-grandmother, and as such, are entitled to income until 1991 when the trust ceases and Ps receive the principal. Ps claimed in the district court that the bank trustee (D) had breached various fiduciary obligations. The court found that D had failed to act impartially as between the trust's income beneficiaries and remaindermen. D sold the trust's real estate at the lowest point of value. Both sides appeal different aspects of the judgment.

Issue. Did D act unfairly as between the income beneficiaries and the remaindermen?

Held. Yes. Judgment affirmed as modified.

- The district court found that D failed to keep up the real estate, to renovate, modernize, or to take other reasonable steps that might have given the remaindermen property roughly capable of continuing to produce reasonable income. The record provides adequate support for these conclusions, and we will not overturn a district court's factual determination unless it is clearly erroneous, particularly in a diversity case where a reasonable construction of state law is involved.

- D did not appraise the property periodically, did not keep proper records, and made no accounting for 55 years. An impartial trustee must view the overall picture, not close its eyes to relevant facts.

- D could have sold the property in 1950 and reinvested the proceeds so as not to create a "partiality" problem. The Restatement (Second) of Trusts says a trustee is under a duty to the beneficiary ultimately entitled to principal not to retain property certain or likely to depreciate, even though the property yields a high income, unless D makes adequate provision for amortizing the income.

- State case law allows the court considerable discretion in fiduciary breach cases to fashion a remedy based on a hypothetical sale. The year 1950 is not an unreasonable remedial choice because that date marks a reasonable outer bound of the time the trustee could plead ignorance of the serious fairness problem.

- The district court's surcharge calculation is approved except for the additional percentage to reflect "appreciation." There is no reason to believe D would have outperformed inflation.

- D's removal is primarily a matter for the district court. D can be removed even if charges of misconduct are not made out. Ill feeling might interfere here with the trust administration.

E. SUBRULES RELATING TO THE TRUST PROPERTY

1. **Duty to Collect and Protect Trust Property.** A trustee has the duty to immediately collect the trust assets and ascertain that the executor has tendered the appropriate property.

2. **Duty to Earmark Trust Property.** A trustee has a duty to earmark property and is liable for any loss that results from the failure to do so.

3. **Duty Not to Mingle Trust Funds with Trustee's Own.** A trustee has a duty to not commingle the trust funds with his own and will be liable for losses resulting from commingling.

F. DUTY TO INFORM AND ACCOUNT TO THE BENEFICIARIES

1. **Full Disclosure Required--**

Fletcher v. Fletcher, 480 S.E.2d 488 (Va. 1997).

Facts. Upon the death of her husband, Elinor Fletcher (T) placed all of her assets in a revocable inter vivos trust for which she was the grantor and trustee. Several years later, she amended the trust to contain, among other things, a provision establishing several trusts upon her death. Three of these trusts ($50,000 each) were for the benefit of her adult son, James (P), and his two children. Another adult son and F & M Bank-Peoples Trust and Asset Management Group (Ds) were appointed successor trustees. The trust for P authorized the trustees to expend such amounts of income and principal necessary to provide him and his children with adequate medical care and insurance for P's life or until his trust is depleted. Upon P's death, any remaining trust balance is to be paid to P's children. Upon T's death, her trust became irrevocable and Ds assumed their duties. P brought a proceeding against Ds to compel Ds to provide full and complete copies of the trust instruments, alleging that T had transferred assets described on a "Schedule A" attached to the original trust instrument to a "new trust" with Ds as trustees and that Ds had failed to provide P with the details of this trust. P further alleged that he was given only certain pages from the original trust and the amendment, and that without a complete listing of the terms and assets of the trust, he cannot determine if the trust is being properly administered. P alleged his brother's claim that their mother wanted the trust kept confidential from the beneficiaries is without documented support. Ds assert that upon T's death, when separate trusts were created, P was provided with all documents that relate to him and his children and was not entitled to any further information. Ds filed the trust agreement under seal with the court, but failed to file "Schedule A." The trial court, after hearing, ruled in favor of P. Ds appeal.

Issue. Did the trial court err in finding that P had an absolute right to the complete copies of the trust agreement and ordering Ds to provide P with same?

Held. No. Judgment affirmed.

♦ While this is a case of first impression in Virginia, we are guided by text writers and the Restatement (Second) of Trusts.

♦ The beneficiaries are the equitable owners of the trust property; the trustees are merely representatives who keep the trust property safe and administer the trust according to the provisions of the trust instrument.

♦ Because the beneficiary enjoys the trust property indirectly, that does not imply the beneficiary is to have the nature of the trust property and its administration kept from him.

♦ "(W)here a trust is created for several beneficiaries, each of them is entitled to information as to the trust." [Scott, The Law of Trusts §173 (4th ed. 1987)]

♦ Even if the trust terms regulate the amount of information the trustee must give and the frequency with which it must be given, the beneficiary is always entitled to as much information as is reasonably necessary to allow him to enforce his rights or prevent a breach.

♦ The trust here contains no provision that P should not be given information and there was no evidentiary hearing below regarding Ds' assertion that T gave oral directions to that purpose. Therefore, we do not opine on what effect any directive of secrecy by the grantor would have here.

♦ Ds' claim that the grantor's creation of three separate trusts somehow make the trust three separate and independent trust documents is without merit. There is one trust agreement based on a "unitary corpus."

♦ The information Ds failed to disclose to P may have a material bearing on the administration of the trust as far as P is concerned. Without full disclosure, P cannot judge Ds' investment decisions and cannot determine whether Ds are carrying out their duty to use reasonable care and skill to make the property productive and are acting impartially.

2. Constructive Fraud--

National Academy of Sciences v. Cambridge Trust Co., 346 N.E.2d 879 (Mass. 1976).

Facts. The will of the decedent, Leonard T. Troland (T), left all of his Cambridge property to be held in trust by the Cambridge Trust Company (D), with the net income to be paid to his wife for life as long as she remained unmarried. It further provided that his wife should not devote any major portion of her income to the support or benefit of people other than herself. T further provided that on his wife's death, D would transfer the trusteeship to the National Research Council of Washington, D.C., an agency of the National Academy of Sciences (P), to constitute a trust for research in psycho-physics. The widow subsequently remarried but failed to notify D of this. The National Academy of Sciences (P) brought a petition seeking a revocation of the accounts of D and restoration by D of the $106,000 that was paid to the widow after her remarriage. The probate court held for P, ordering revocation of the accounts and charging D for the amounts erroneously distributed. D appeals.

Issue. Does the failure to make any reasonable effort to ascertain the true set of facts constitute a sufficient basis on which to hold a trustee responsible for a constructive fraud on beneficiaries of a trust?

Held. Yes. Judgment affirmed.

♦ If a person makes a representation of fact in relation to subject matter susceptible of knowledge and such representation is not true, and if another party to whom it is made relies and acts upon it, it is fraud and deceit for which the party making it is responsible. We hold that the "fraud" in the applicable statute contemplates this standard of constructive fraud, at least to the extent that the fiduciary has made no reasonable efforts to ascertain the true state of facts that it has misrepresented in the accounts. Here, the probate court found that D made no effort at all to ascertain if the widow had remarried.

XIV. WEALTH TRANSFER TAXATION: TAX PLANNING

A. INTRODUCTION

1. **A Brief History of the Federal Estate Tax.** In 1916, Congress established an estate tax, which is imposed on the estate of a decedent. To prevent the avoidance of death taxes by inter vivos gifts, Congress imposed a gift tax in 1931.

    a. **Revisions.** Under the Tax Reform Act of 1976, Congress united the gift and estate taxes, and the same rate schedule was applied to both gifts and estates. The federal estate and gift tax system was completely revised under the Economic Recovery Tax Act of 1981. This act increased the tax exemption to $600,000, expanded the unified credit, introduced an unlimited marital deduction, and reduced the maximum rate bracket from 70% to 50%.

        1) **The Tax Reform Act of 1986.** The Tax Reform Act of 1986 did away with the exemption of the life estate from estate taxation and imposed a generation-skipping transfer ("GST") tax at the highest rate of the estate tax upon any generation-skipping transfer. Before this act, it was possible to avoid federal estate taxation by creating trusts at death that provided successive life estates for each succeeding generation, because federal estate taxes were not imposed on property in which a descendent only had a life estate. Through the GST tax, the government tried to carry out a policy of imposing an estate tax at least once as wealth passed from one generation to the next.

        2) **The Economic Growth and Tax Relief Reconciliation Act of 2001 ("EGTRRA").** The EGTRRA phased in the repeal of the estate tax by increasing the exemption amount and decreasing the top tax rate. However, due to budget constraints and political compromise, the estate and GST taxes are actually repealed for only one year—2010, and the gift tax remains to prevent avoidance of the income tax. If there is no further action, the 2001 amendments will sunset, and on January 1, 2011, all wealth transfer taxes will revert to their pre-2001 state.

2. **Estate and Inheritance Taxes Distinguished.** An estate tax is a tax upon the value of all property owned by a decedent that is transferred to the decedent's heirs or beneficiaries upon the decedent's death. On the other hand, an inheritance tax is a tax upon the value of property received by an heir or beneficiary for the privilege of receiving the property from the dead.

3. **The Unified Federal Estate and Gift Taxes.** Under the unified system, unified taxes are imposed on the estates of decedents dying after December 31, 1976, and for gifts made after that date. The rates are progressive based on cumulative lifetime and death transfers.

4. **Liability for Payment of Taxes.**

   a. **Payment of gift tax.** The donor is primarily liable for payment of the gift tax. However, if the donor fails to pay the tax, the donee is liable for any unpaid gift tax.

   b. **Payment of estate tax.** The executor or administrator of a decedent's estate is personally liable for payment of the tax until she has been discharged from liability, but she is generally entitled to reimbursement out of the decedent's estate.

B. THE FEDERAL GIFT TAX

1. **Nature of a Taxable Gift.** Section 2501(a) of the Internal Revenue Code of 1986 levies a gift tax upon the transfer of property by gift. The courts have held that a "gift" occurs when the donor relinquishes complete dominion and control. In a revocable trust, a taxable transfer does not occur until the power of revocation ceases.

   a. **Discretionary power in trustee--**

Holtz's Estate v. Commissioner, 38 T.C. 37 (1962).

Facts. A trust instrument of the decedent, Leon Holtz, provided that the trustee should distribute the net income to the settlor as the trustee thinks desirable, and upon the settlor's death, if his wife survived him, the income of the trust should be paid to her for life, and upon the death of both the settlor and his wife, the trust would terminate and the remaining principal would be paid to the estate of the survivor. The settlor transferred property having a value of $384,000 into the trust and thereafter he transferred an additional $50,000 to the trust. The Commissioner (D) determined that as a result of these transfers, Holtz made taxable gifts in the amount of $263,000, which were subject to the gift tax. The settlor's estate (P) petitions the court and contends that the transfers were not completed gifts and that no part thereof was subject to the gift tax.

Issue. Does the placing of discretionary power in the trustee to invade corpus make the gift of corpus incomplete and hence not subject to the gift tax?

Held. Yes. Decision for P.

♦   The placing of discretionary power in the trustee to invade the corpus makes the gift of the corpus incomplete under certain circumstances. The rule of thumb is generally that if the trustee is free to exercise his unfettered discretion and there is nothing to compel him to invade the corpus, then the settlor retains a mere expectancy that does not make the gift incomplete. However, if the exercise of the trustee's discretion is governed by some external standard that a court may apply in compelling compliance with the conditions of the trust agreement, and the trustee's power to invade is unlimited, then the gift of corpus is incomplete.

♦ Here, the trustee had unfettered power to use all of the corpus for the benefit of the settlor if it thought that it was desirable for the welfare, comfort, and needs of the settlor. It is reasonable to assume that the trustee would, and could be required to, invade the corpus if this was desirable for the welfare, comfort, and needs of the settlor. It was thus possible that the entire corpus might be distributed during the settlor's lifetime. Hence, the settlor had not abandoned sufficient dominion and control over the property transferred to make the gift consummate.

---

      b.   **Income tax basis.** Under the federal income tax, a tax is imposed upon capital gain from the sale of property. The amount of the tax varies according to the amount of gain, which is the difference between the "basis" and the selling price.

2.   **The Annual Exclusion.** Under section 2503(b) of the Code, a taxpayer may exclude from taxable gifts the first $10,000 given to any person during the year. In Congress's 1997 Amendment to the Code, the exclusion was indexed for inflation. The exclusion now increases in $1,000 increments as the cost of living rises. The Code also provides an unlimited exclusion for tuition fees and medical expenses paid on behalf of another. The annual exclusion is not applicable to gifts of future interests.

      a.   **Transfer for the benefit of minor.** Section 2503(c) of the Code provides a way to avoid having a gift to a minor classified as a future interest. An annual exclusion for property transferred to a trust for a minor is authorized if all the property and the income therefrom may be expended for the benefit of the minor before he attains age 21, as long as the property and any accumulated income will be distributed to the minor at age 21 or, if the child dies before attaining age 21, to his estate or appointee.

      b.   **Gifts of a present interest in property--**

Estate of Cristofani v. Commissioner, 97 T.C. 74 (1991).

Facts. The decedent, Maria Cristofani (T), had two children (Cs) and five grandchildren (Gs). T executed an irrevocable trust; Cs were trustees. Both Cs and Gs had the right under the trust terms, during a 15-day period following a contribution, to withdraw an amount not to exceed the amount specified for the federal gift tax exclusion under section

2503(b). Cs could apply as much of the principal as necessary for their proper support, health, maintenance, and education, taking into account several factors including T's desire to consider Cs the primary beneficiaries and Gs the secondary beneficiaries. T intended to fund the trust with a one-third individual interest in certain real property for 1984, 1985, and 1986. T did this for two years, transferring an interest valued at $70,000 each year. T died prior to making the 1986 transfer. T did not report the transfers on federal gift tax returns. T claimed seven annual exclusions under section 2503(b) for 1984 and 1985 with respect to Cs and Gs. Gs did not exercise their rights to withdraw under the trust during those years. The IRS (D) allowed T's estate (P) to claim the exclusions with respect to Cs but disallowed it for Gs for 1984 and 1985, determining that Gs' claimed exclusions were not transfers of present interests. P appeals.

Issue. Do transfers of property to a trust, where the beneficiaries possess the right to withdraw an amount not in excess of the section 2503(b) exclusion within 15 days of such transfers, constitute gifts of a present interest in property within the meaning of section 2503(b)?

Held. Yes. Decision entered for P.

♦ For purposes of the exclusion, a trust beneficiary is considered a donee of a gift in trust.

♦ The exclusion applies to present interests in property, an unrestricted right to the immediate use, possession, or enjoyment of property or income from property.

♦ In *Crummey v. Commissioner,* 397 F.2d 82 (9th Cir. 1968), the court focused on the minor beneficiaries' legal right to demand payment from the trustee, not on the likelihood that they would actually receive present enjoyment of the property. If the beneficiaries had a legal right to make a demand upon the trustee that could not be resisted, the court determined the beneficiaries received a present interest.

♦ Revenue rulings are not authority for this court but this ruling shows the IRS's recognition of what constitutes a present interest.

♦ Here, the exclusions were allowed for Cs, who possessed the same right of withdrawal as Gs. Gs' legal right to withdraw specified amounts constitutes a gift of a present interest.

♦ It is not required that trust beneficiaries have a vested present interest or a vested remainder interest in the trust corpus or income in order to qualify for the exclusion.

---

3. **Gifts Between Spouses and from One Spouse to a Third Person.** Under the Economic Recovery Tax Act of 1981, a husband and wife may transfer their property to each other without the payment of any transfer taxes. However, when the assets pass to a third person, a transfer tax is imposed.

C. THE FEDERAL ESTATE TAX

1. **Introduction.** The federal estate tax taxes the value of property owned or passing at death and the value of property given away during life.

2. **The Gross Estate: Property Passing by Will or Intestacy.**

   a. **Section 2033: Property owned at death.** Under this section, the value of the gross estate includes the value of property to the extent of the decedent's interest at the time of death; it includes all property owned at death that passes by will or intestacy. It does not reach a decedent's life estate created by another person.

   b. **Section 2034: Dower or curtesy.** Section 2034 of the Code includes in a decedent's gross estate "the value of all property to the extent of any interest therein of the surviving spouse, existing at the time of the decedent's death as dower or curtesy, or by virtue of a statute creating an estate in lieu of dower or curtesy." This does not apply to community property. In community property states, on the death of either spouse only that spouse's half is includable in the gross estate; the other half belongs to the surviving spouse and is not includable. Note that the importance of section 2034 is greatly offset by the marital deduction, which operates to take out of the taxable estate most of the property included therein under section 2034.

3. **The Gross Estate: Nonprobate Property.**

   a. **Section 2040: Joint tenancy.**

      1) **Joint tenancy between persons other than husband and wife.** Under section 2040(a), the entire value of the property held in joint tenancy, except that part attributable to the amount of consideration furnished by the other joint tenant, must be included.

      2) **Joint tenancy and tenancy by the entirety between husband and wife.** Under section 2040(b), half the value of property held by the decedent and the decedent's spouse as joint tenants with right of survivorship or as tenants by the entirety is includable in the decedent's gross estate. It does not matter which spouse furnished the consideration for the property's acquisition. Since each spouse is deemed to own half of the amount of the joint tenancy with right of survivorship or tenancy by the entirety, the decedent's spouse's half interest in the property included in the gross estate will receive a stepped-up basis at death.

   b. **Section 2039: Employee death benefits.** Under section 2039, the value of amounts receivable by a beneficiary under an agreement where the decedent, during life, was receiving or had a right to receive payments is included in the decedent's estate. Death benefits are not includable in the decedent's estate if he is prevented from selecting the beneficiary because, for example, a statute requires the benefits to be payable to his spouse or children. If benefits are payable to a beneficiary at a scheduled time or upon the happening of an event, irrespective of whether the decedent is living or dead, they are not taxable under section 2039, even though the decedent may be dead at the time scheduled for payment.

    c.   **Section 2042: Life insurance.** Under section 2042, a decedent's gross estate includes the value of any life insurance proceeds if the decedent possessed at death any of the incidents of ownership under the policies or if the policy proceeds were payable to the insured's executor or estate.

4.   **The Gross Estate: Lifetime Transfers.**

    a.   **Section 2036: Transfers with life estate or power of control retained.** Section 2036(a)(1) applies to property transferred during the decedent's lifetime if the decedent retained a life estate in the transferred property. The transfer is subject to estate taxation because the decedent retained the right to possess and enjoy the property or the right to income from it until his death. Section 2036(a)(2) exposes to estate tax any property transferred by the decedent wherein there was retained the right, either alone or in conjunction with another person, to control the beneficial enjoyment of the property or income therefrom. The tax will attach despite the fact that the transferor could not have exercised the power so as to secure a personal economic benefit.

        1)   **No bona fide sale--**

Estate of Maxwell v. Commissioner, 3 F.3d 591 (2d Cir. 1993).

Facts. The decedent, Lydia Maxwell (T), conveyed her home to her son and his wife in 1984 for $270,000. T leased the premises for five years at $1,800 per month. T forgave $20,000 of the purchase price as part of the annual gift tax exclusion and held a mortgage for the remaining $250,000. The buyers paid expenses. The rent essentially canceled out the mortgage payments, and the buyers were never called upon to pay mortgage principal. Upon T's death, the buyers sold the home for $550,000. On T's estate tax return, the estate (P) reported $210,000 remaining on the mortgage debt. The Commissioner (D) found that the 1984 transaction constituted a transfer with a retained life estate and assessed a deficiency to adjust for the difference between the fair market value and the reported amount. P appealed to the tax court, which affirmed D. P appeals.

Issues.

(i)   Did T retain possession or enjoyment of the property following the transfer?

(ii)   If she did, was the transfer a bona fide sale for an adequate and full consideration in money or money's worth?

Held. (i) Yes. (ii) No. Judgment affirmed.

♦ Section 2036(a) requires inclusion in the value of the gross estate of all property transferred under which the decedent retained a life estate, *i.e.,* possession, enjoyment, or right to income from the property.

♦ Possession or enjoyment is retained when there is an express or implied understanding to that effect among the parties to the transfer.

♦ The mortgage note had no value if there was, as the tax court determined from the conduct of the parties, no intention that it would ever be paid.

♦ The forgiveness of the initial $20,000 strongly suggests the existence of an understanding between T and the buyers that T would forgive $20,000 each year until her death and the balance would be forgiven by T's will.

---

2) Requirement of an ascertainable standard--

Old Colony Trust Co. v. United States, 423 F.2d 601 (1st Cir. 1970).

Facts. The decedent had established a trust for the benefit of his son and named himself as a trustee. The trust permitted the trustees to increase the percentage of income payable to the son beyond the prescribed 80% when in their opinion such increase was needed in case of sickness or was desirable in view of changed circumstances. In addition, the trustees were given the discretion to cease paying income to the son. Another article gave broad administrative and management powers to the trustees. A deficiency was assessed against the estate. The executor (P) paid the tax and sued for its recovery in district court. The court ruled for the government (D). Old Colony Trust Company appeals.

Issue. If there is no ascertainable standard with which a settlor-trustee must comply in his distribution of trust income, will the settlor's estate be taxed according to the value of the principal that the settlor contributed?

Held. Yes. Judgment affirmed.

♦ If there is an ascertainable standard, the trustee can be compelled to follow it. If there is not, even though he is a fiduciary, it is not unreasonable to say that his retention of an unmeasurable freedom of choice is equivalent to retaining some of the incidents of ownership. Hence, if there is an ascertainable standard, the settlor-trustee's estate is not taxed, but if there is not, it is taxed.

♦ Here, the settlor retained the unrestricted power to distribute the trust income. Accordingly, the tax was properly assessed.

b. **Section 2038: Revocable transfers.** Under section 2038, the value of the gross estate includes the value of all property "of which the decedent has at any time made a transfer . . . by trust or otherwise, where the enjoyment thereof was subject . . . to any change through the [decedent's] exercise of a power . . . to alter, amend, revoke or terminate. . . ." Unless the decedent has the right to exercise the power, a transfer subject to such power is not taxable in her estate. This is true even if the power is vested in one who lacks a substantial adverse interest to the decedent, such as a trustee or even a subordinate party (*e.g.,* transferor's spouse).

c. **Section 2037: Transfers with reversionary interest retained.** Under section 2037, the decedent's gross estate includes the value of property transferred during his life if (i) possession can only be obtained by surviving the decedent, (ii) the decedent reserved a reversionary interest in the property, and (iii) that reversionary interest was worth more than 5% of the value of the property immediately before the decedent died.

5. **Section 2035: Transfers Within Three Years of Death.** Under section 2035, certain inter vivos transfers made within three years prior to death are brought within the decedent's gross estate.

6. **The Gross Estate: Powers of Appointment.** Under section 2041, the gross estate includes the value of property over which the decedent held a general power of appointment at the time of her death. The owner of a general power of appointment is considered the owner of the property subject to the power. When the general power of appointment is exercised or released, the donee has made a taxable gift. If the decedent merely possessed a general power of appointment at the time of her death, the property is taxable whether or not the power was exercised. Property subject solely to a special power is not taxable in the donee's estate under section 2041.

a. **Comfort limited by ascertainable standard--**

Estate of Vissering v. Commissioner, 990 F.2d 578 (10th Cir. 1993).

Facts. The mother of the decedent, Norman Vissering (T), created a trust controlled by Florida law. T and a bank served as co-trustees. T received all the income from the trust after his mother's death and on T's death the assets were to be divided in equal parts for T's two children. T developed Alzheimer's disease and entered a nursing home in 1984 but never resigned as trustee. At T's death, he possessed a power of appointment that permitted him to benefit himself, his estate, his creditors or the estate's creditors for his "continued comfort." The tax court held that T held at his death a general power defined by I.R.C. section 2041, requiring the trust assets to be included in T's gross estate. T's estate appeals.

Issue. Did T hold powers permitting him to invade the principal of the trust for his own benefit, unrestrained by an ascertainable standard relating to health, education, support, or maintenance?

Held. No. Judgment reversed and remanded.

♦ State law determines legal interests and rights created by the trust instrument, but federal law determines tax consequences.

♦ Florida law would hold that a trust document permitting invasion of principal for "comfort," without qualifying language, creates a general power of appointment.

♦ However, there is modifying language in the trust here—"to the extent required for continued comfort"—that we believe would lead Florida to hold does not permit an unlimited power of invasion.

♦ Examples in the Treasury Regulation, such as "support in reasonable comfort," "maintenance in health and reasonable comfort," and "support in his accustomed manner of living," deemed to be limited by an ascertainable standard are no different from the language in T's trust provision.

♦ If T sought to use the trust assets to significantly increase his standard of living, his co-trustee would have been obligated to withhold consent and the remainder beneficiaries could have petitioned the court to disallow such expenditures as inconsistent with the settlor's intent.

---

b.   **Sequential trusts--**

Estate of Kurz v. Commissioner, 68 F.3d 1027 (7th Cir. 1995).

Facts. Between 1971 (the year of her husband's death) and 1986, Ethel Kurz was the income beneficiary of two trusts. From the marital trust, she was entitled to as much principal as she wanted by written request to the trustees. From the family trust, she was entitled to 5% of the principal in any year only if the marital trust was exhausted. Upon Kurz's death in 1986, the marital trust was worth $3.5 million and the family trust $3.4 million. The estate tax return included the full value of the marital trust but none of the value of the family trust. The IRS assessed additional estate taxes. The estate (P) challenged the assessment. The tax court held that Kurz held a general power of appointment over 5% of the family trust and another $170,000 should be included in her estate under 26 U.S.C. section 2041(a)(2). P appeals.

Issue. Does a sequence of withdrawal rights prevent a power of appointment from being exercisable?

Held. No. Judgment affirmed.

♦ Section 2041 is designed to include in the taxable estate all assets possessed or controlled by the decedent.

♦ If only a condition the decedent could have controlled had to be satisfied to receive the money from the family trust, then the decedent's power is exercisable.

♦ P erroneously relies on the regulations accompanying section 2041, and in particular, one statement: "[A] power which by its terms is exercisable only upon the occurrence during the decedent's lifetime of an event or a contingency which did not in fact take place or occur during such time is not a power in existence on the date of the decedent's death." P's claim that the required "contingency" did not occur here fails. The examples of contingencies following this sentence (if a decedent reached a certain age, if a decedent survived another person, or if she died without descendants) are outside of the decedent's control. Expediently arranging trusts in a sequence and arranging a sequence of withdrawal does not create a contingency and does not remove the beneficiary's dominion and control over all funds that can be withdrawn at any given moment.

---

7. **The Marital Deduction.**

   a. **Introduction.** Under section 2056, spouses may transfer between themselves unlimited amounts of property (except terminable interests) without incurring any gift or estate taxes.

   b. **Interests that qualify for the deduction.** For an interest to qualify as a marital deduction, the following requirements must be met:

      (i)   The decedent was a citizen of the United States;

      (ii) The decedent was survived by his spouse;

      (iii) The value of the interest deducted is includable in the decedent's gross estate;

      (iv) The interest passes to the surviving spouse; and

      (v)   The interest is a deductible interest (*i.e.,* the interest passing to the surviving spouse is subject to taxation in her estate to the extent not consumed or disposed of during her lifetime).

      1) **Failure to qualify for the deduction--**

Estate of Rapp v. Commissioner, 140 F.3d 1211 (9th Cir. 1998).

Facts. When the testator, Bert Rapp (T), died, survived by a wife and two children, he willed all of his household and personal property to his wife and one-half of the community property to a trust for his wife for her life. T's children, as co-trustees, were given absolute discretion to distribute from the principal and income such amounts as they determined necessary for their mother's health, education, and support. Upon the wife's death, the remaining trust assets, if any, were to be distributed among T's children and their issue. Upon T's death, Mrs. Rapp asked the probate court to modify the will so the above provision would qualify for the marital deduction. She alleged that it was T's intention that the income from the trust would be paid to Mrs. Rapp at least annually, or during her lifetime. California law allows the court to modify or terminate a trust upon the consent of all parties or due to changed circumstances. After a hearing of which the IRS did not receive notice and during which no witnesses were called, the court granted Mrs. Rapp's petition and entered an order changing the language of the trust so as to authorize the executor to treat the trust as a qualified terminable interest property ("QTIP") trust. The order became final and unappealable on April 30, 1989. After the order was entered, but before it was final, the executor (P) filed with the IRS (D) an application for an extension of time to file the estate tax return. P indicated on the application that he intended to make a QTIP election and he submitted an estimated payment of $156,204. The return was filed in May, after the order became final, and P claimed the QTIP deduction for $3,683,899, as much of the estate as would bring the taxes to the amount he had previously paid. D sent a deficiency notice, claiming P failed to provide full substantiation for the deduction and it would be allowed only for the value of the household and personal goods that had passed directly to Mrs. Rapp, *i.e.*, $435,262.50. P appealed. The tax court claimed that the California court's decision had not been affirmed by the California Supreme Court and was not binding, that the probate court had erred, and that the trust was not a QTIP trust. P appeals.

Issues.

(i)   Does the trust created by T's will constitute a QTIP trust, which qualifies for the marital tax deduction?

(ii)   Is the tax court bound by the California probate court's reformation of T's will?

Held. (i) No. (ii) No. Judgment affirmed.

♦   *Internal Revenue v. Estate of Bosch*, 387 U.S. 456 (1967), is controlling with regard to the effect of the state court's determination. In reviewing the legislative history of the marital deduction statute, the *Bosch* court determined that Congress intended that "proper regard" be given a state court's interpretation after a "bona fide adversary proceeding," but not finality. Congress did not intend the state courts to determine federal law.

♦   While the probate court's order was final and cannot be overruled by the California Supreme Court, this has no effect on the fact that the federal court is not bound by state court proceedings for determining federal estate taxes. The state court reformation is still in effect for Mrs. Rapp, but she will not receive QTIP benefits.

---

2) Reformation allowed--

Pond v. Pond, 678 N.E.2d 1321 (Mass. 1997).

Facts. In 1991, the settlor, Sidney Pond (T), executed his will leaving all of his personal property to his wife and the residue to a revocable trust, naming himself and his wife trustees, executed on the same day. All of their assets except the family home were transferred to the trust. The trust provided that income and such principal as necessary be paid to T and his wife during their lives, but made no provision for any type of payment to his wife if she survived him. The trust provided that it would terminate on the death of both trustees and its assets were to be divided equally between their children. The will provided that the wife had absolute discretion whether or not to elect to qualify under section 2056 (b)(7) all or a portion of the trust for the federal and any state marital deduction. However, section 2056(b)(7) requires income to be paid to the surviving spouse for life in order to qualify for the marital deduction. Without this deduction, the estate would be liable for $70,000 in taxes. Trustee (P) alleges that a scrivener's error is apparent when the estate plan is viewed as a whole and that T intended to provide for his wife. P asks the court to insert into the trust a provision granting the wife trust income and discretionary principal payments for her lifetime. P further requests that the court incorporate into the trust language that would correct the ambiguity in the termination provisions. All beneficiaries (Ds) assent to the requested reformation.

Issue. Should the trust be reformed to give effect to T's intent?

Held. Yes. So ordered.

♦ Clear and decisive proof of mistake is required to reform a trust instrument to embody a settlor's intent.

♦ Both the will and trust were executed on the same day; the trust was clearly intended to provide for the marital deduction. It was essential to the estate plan. All of T's assets were transferred to it. The income and principal were available to T and his wife during their lives. Clearly, T intended the same to continue after his death. Only a scrivener's error could have caused the requisite clause to be omitted. There is no indication that T intended to deprive his wife of the trust assets during her lifetime.

---

c.   **Tax planning.** Each spouse is entitled to one exemption from estate and gift tax, in the form of a unified credit. By taking advantage of both spouses' exemptions, the combined credit can be passed to the couple's children without incurring estate taxes. Because of the graduated tax rates, the total estate tax payable on the death of a husband and wife will be lower if the two estates are equal. Equalization is not necessarily the best solution in all cases. Formula clauses remain useful in producing precisely the right amount to put in a credit shelter trust or a marital deduction trust. A credit shelter trust is a trust designed to hold an amount equal to the exemption of the first spouse to die (*i.e.,* the amount not taxable on his death) in such a manner as not to be taxable on the surviving spouse's death.

8.   **The Charitable Deduction.** Under section 2055 of the Code, unlimited deductions may be taken for transfers for public, charitable, or religious purposes.

D.   THE GENERATION-SKIPPING TAX

The Tax Reform Act of 1986 prevents wealthy persons from creating inter vivos or testamentary trusts for the purpose of avoiding estate or gift taxes. The underlying principle of the generation-skipping transfer tax is that a transfer tax should be imposed once a generation and cannot be avoided by giving the next generation only a life estate or nothing at all. If a trust creates a generation-skipping transfer, the tax is due when the transfer occurs. The transfers are taxed at a flat rate, which is the highest rate applicable. The type of transfer determines the amount taxed and who is liable for payment. Under section 2631(a), an exemption of up to $1 million may be taken by each individual making generation-skipping transfers. A married couple may give away up to $2 million in generation-skipping transfers without having to pay a tax.

E.   STATE WEALTH TRANSFER TAXES

Before the enactment of the Economic Growth and Tax Relief Reconciliation Act of 2001 ("EGTRRA"), estates were allowed a credit against the federal estate tax for death taxes paid to the state. The credit allowed diversion of federal revenues to the state without increasing the tax burden on the state's residents. The EGTRRA began phasing out the federal estate tax credit for state death taxes. Beginning in 2005, the credit was replaced with a deduction (which is not as beneficial as a credit) for state death taxes. Because the EGTRRA may sunset at the end of 2010 (*see* A.1.a.2) *supra*), the future of the federal estate tax and state wealth transfer taxes is uncertain.

TABLE OF CASES
(Page numbers of briefed cases in bold)